At Issue

| Reality TV

Other Books in the At Issue Series:

At Issue

| Reality TV

Thomas Riggs & Company, Book Editor

GREENHAVEN PRESS

A part of Gale, Cengage Learning

GALE
CENGAGE Learning·

Detroit • New York • San Francisco • New Haven, Conn • Waterville, Maine • London

Elizabeth Des Chenes, *Director, Publishing Solutions*

For more information, contact:
Greenhaven Press
27500 Drake Rd.
Farmington Hills, MI 48331-3535
Or you can visit our Internet site at gale.cengage.com

Articles in Greenhaven Press anthologies are often edited for length to meet page requirements. In addition, original titles of these works are changed to clearly present the main thesis and to explicitly indicate the author's opinion. Every effort is made to ensure that Greenhaven Press accurately reflects the original intent of the authors. Every effort has been made to trace the owners of copyrighted material.

Cover photograph reproduced by permission of Brand X Pictures.

LIBRARY OF CONGRESS CATALOGING-IN-PUBLICATION DATA

Reality TV / Thomas Riggs & Company, book editor.
    p. cm. -- (At issue)
  Includes bibliographical references and index.
  ISBN 978-0-7377-6195-5 (hardcover) -- ISBN 978-0-7377-6196-2 (pbk.)
  1. Reality television programs--History and criticism. 2. Reality television programs--Social aspects. I. Riggs, Thomas, 1963-
  PN1992.8.R43R455 2013
  791.45'6--dc23
                                                          2012049714

Printed in the United States of America
1 2 3 4 5 6 7 17 16 15 14 13

Contents

Introduction

Around the turn of the twenty-first century, subtle changes began to take shape in the American television landscape. While scripted dramas like *ER, The Practice*, and *Law & Order* and comedies like *Friends, Frasier*, and *Everybody Loves Raymond* remained among the most popular shows of the era, a new show, *Survivor*, surprised producers and critics alike by becoming the single most-watched program of the 2000–2001 season. Combining elements of a popular game show genre (*Who Wants to Be a Millionaire* had captured the top position for the previous season) with athletic competition, social experiment, and documentary filmmaking, *Survivor* averaged more than twenty-eight million viewers in its first season, remaining among the ten most-watched programs through the 2005–2006 season, and in the top twenty well into the following decade.

Although the show's use of competition as a central feature was a new twist, *Survivor* was not the first show to place strangers in unique situations in the hopes of capturing spontaneous, compelling storylines. MTV's *The Real World*, billed as "the true story of seven strangers picked to live in a house, work together and have their lives taped to find out what happens when people stop being polite and start getting real," debuted in 1992. It rapidly gained popularity as cast members explored important social and political issues of the day—especially among the coveted 18–24 age group—through their everyday conversations and interactions. While some critics suggest that the reality TV genre stems back to the 1973 PBS documentary series *An American Family*, for most the arrival of *The Real World* and its 1995 spinoff, *Road Rules*, marks the beginning of the reality TV era, while the debut of *Survivor* signifies its crossover to mainstream appeal.

Since 2000, reality television has proliferated like no other genre before it, spawning numerous subgenres and greatly increasing viewership for cable channels like *E!, A&E, Bravo,* and *TLC,* once considered niche channels intended for a specific subset of viewers only. Today nearly five hundred reality programs are aired across the network and cable spectrum each year, filling out a number of different categories, including competition, dating, occupational, self-improvement, renovation, and social experiment shows. In the 2011–2012 season, three reality competition shows, *American Idol, Dancing with the Stars,* and *The Voice,* claimed five spots on the list of ten most-watched programs. Such programs as *Keeping Up with the Kardashians, Jersey Shore,* and the numerous iterations of the *Real Housewives* franchise have influenced all aspects of popular culture and introduced the contemporary phenomenon of "being famous for being famous" by manufacturing celebrities seemingly out of thin air. What appeared to be an anomaly in 2000 has evolved into an entertainment juggernaut and a multi-billion-dollar industry, leaving few viewers without an opinion on the genre's merits.

Among viewers, reality television has a wide appeal for a variety of reasons. For some, it provides a window into different cultures and lifestyles with shows like *Swamp People, Sister Wives, Little People Big World, Jersey Shore,* and *All American Muslim,* offering glimpses of unique subsets of American society. For others, reality programs such as *Teen Mom, Celebrity Rehab, Hoarders, Intervention, The Biggest Loser,* and *True Life* explore relevant and often underexposed challenges faced by ordinary people. Still others find inspiration and hope in seeing ordinary people attain nationwide recognition for their talents on shows like *America's Got Talent, The X Factor, America's Next Top Model, Top Chef,* and *Project Runway.* Finally, some see the genre as entertainment plain and simple, finding more riveting drama in *The Real Housewives of Orange County* than in any scripted program.

Television producers also have plenty to like about the genre: most significantly, the unscripted nature of reality programs and lack of emphasis on visual quality means that a season's worth of reality programming can be completed with a fraction of the production crew and at a fraction of the cost of traditional scripted programming. Reality shows flourished during the 2007–2008 Writers Guild of America strike, as producers and executives scrambled to find programming to replace the suddenly halted scripted shows. Cast members, too, often reap benefits from their participation. Winning contestants on talent competition shows can kick-start a career in the performing arts; charismatic participants in social experiment shows build a personal "brand" that lends itself toward a future as a spokesperson or on-air personality; former celebrities can reinvigorate or redefine their careers by appearing on a reality program.

Yet, for all of its appeal, reality television is mired in controversy. Because the genre is so dependent on creating and maintaining compelling storylines predicated on interpersonal conflict, participants are often pigeonholed into a variety of unflattering stereotypes through creative—some say manipulative—editing. Some, like *The Apprentice*'s notorious villain, Omarosa Manigault, embrace their character type and turn it to their advantage. But many psychologists argue that the pressures of appearing on a reality show, of living one's life in front of a camera and under constant public scrutiny, can lead participants to lose touch with their identity and ultimately spiral into depression, particularly when the cameras are no longer there. The 2011 suicide of Russell Armstrong, the former husband of *Real Housewives of Beverly Hills* star Taylor Armstrong, whose marital and financial problems were put on display in the show's first season, brought this issue into sharp focus and served as the catalyst for debate over the exploitation of reality TV participants. The effect of reality shows on viewers—particularly those under the age of eighteen who often seek to emulate the combative and self-serving behavior of the most recognizable reality characters—is also a major concern to critics who blame the genre for a general decline in civic decency and intelligent discourse.

Whether you view reality television as an important and innovative revolution in the way we tell stories and explore human nature or as a breeding ground for exploitation and demeaning racial, sexual, cultural, and gender stereotypes is largely a matter of personal taste and perspective. With convincing arguments on either side of the debate, many of which are represented in the following volume, there appears to be little chance of reaching a general consensus. But with scores of reality shows debuting with each new season, it becomes increasingly clear that the reality genre has altered the face of television and will continue to capture the public attention in the years to come.

Reality Television Benefits Society More than Scripted Television Does

Michael Hirschorn

Michael Hirschorn is a contributing editor for the Atlantic *and the head of Ish Entertainment, a production company specializing in unscripted television. He was formerly vice president of original programming for VH1, where he helped develop a number of popular reality shows.*

Reality television combines the best elements of documentary film and scripted television while avoiding the problems inherent in each. Like documentary film, it explores controversial issues and provides valuable insight into the lives of others. Like scripted TV, it frames each episode in an overarching narrative that tells an interesting story. But its unscripted format elicits "emotional truths" that are more moving and realistic than anything scripted television can produce, and its observations are more objective than most contemporary documentaries, which often argue for a specific viewpoint.

This past January [2007], I had the pleasure of serving as official spear-catcher for a *CBS Evening News* report on the increasing levels of humiliation on *American Idol* (AI) and other reality-TV shows, including some on my channel, VH1. The segment featured snippets of our shows *I Love New York* (a dating competition with an urban vibe) and *Celebrity Fit Club* (which tracks the efforts of overweight singers and actors to get back in shape, and, by extension, reignite their careers). "VH1, among other things, showcases faded celebrities who are fat," said the CBS correspondent Richard Schlesinger.

In between shots of me fake working at my computer and fake chatting with the amiable Schlesinger while fake strolling down our corporate-looking hallway, I took my best shot at defending the alleged horrors of *AI* and *Celebrity Fit Club*. But it was clear that CBS News was set on bemoaning what it saw as yet another outrage against the culture. The central complaint, per Katie Couric's intro to the report, was that more people had watched *American Idol* the previous week than watched the State of the Union address on all the broadcast networks combined. When the segment ended, Couric signed off with an extravagant eye roll. "We're doing our part here at CBS News," she seemed to be saying, "but the barbarians are massing at the gates, people." A line had been drawn in the sand, as if the news were now akin to an evening at the Met.

The current boom may be a product of the changing economics of the television business, but reality TV is also the liveliest genre on the set right now.

Is there an easier position to take in polite society than to patronize reality TV? Even television programmers see the genre as a kind of visual Hamburger Helper: cheap filler that saves them money they can use elsewhere for more-worthy programming. Reality shows cost anywhere from a quarter to half as much to produce as scripted shows. The money saved on *Extreme Makeover: Home Edition*, the logic goes, allows ABC to pay for additional gruesome medical emergencies and exploding ferries on *Grey's Anatomy*. NBC's crappy *Fear Factor* pays for the classy *Heroes*.

Television's Liveliest Genre

As befits a form driven largely by speed and cost consider-ations, reality TV is not often formally daring. Fifteen years after MTV's *The Real World* set the template for contemporary reality TV by placing seven strangers in a downtown Manhat-tan loft, reality television has developed its own visual short-hand: short doses of documentary footage interspersed with testimonials (often called OTFs, for "on-the-fly" interviews) in which the participants describe, ex post facto, what they were thinking during the action you are watching.

The current boom may be a product of the changing eco-nomics of the television business, but reality TV is also the liveliest genre on the set right now. It has engaged hot-button cultural issues—class, sex, race—that respectable television, including the august *CBS Evening News,* rarely touches. And it has addressed a visceral need for a different kind of television at a time when the Web has made more traditionally pro-duced video seem as stagey as [seventeenth-century French playwright] Molière.

Reality TV may be an awkward admixture of documentary (with its connotations of thousands of hours of footage pa-tiently gathered, redacted by monk-like figures into the purest expression of truth possible in 90 to 120 minutes) and scripted (with its auteurs and Emmys and noble overtones of craft). But this kludge also happens to have allowed reality shows to skim the best elements of scripted TV and documentaries while eschewing the problems of each. Reality shows steal the story structure and pacing of scripted television, but leave be-hind the canned plots and characters. They have the visceral impact of documentary reportage without the self-importance and general lugubriousness. Where documentaries must con-struct their narratives from found matter, reality TV can place real people in artificial surroundings designed for maximum emotional impact.

Scripted television is supposedly showing new ambition these days, particularly in the hour-long drama form. *Studio 60 on the Sunset Strip* was going to bring the chatty intelligence of *The West Wing* back to prime time. *Lost* was going to challenge network audiences like never before, with complex plots, dozens of recurring characters, and movie-level production values. Shows are bigger now: On *24* this season, a nuclear bomb exploded. But network prime-time television remains dominated by variants on the police procedural (*Law & Order, CSI, Criminal Minds*), in which a stock group of characters (ethnically, sexually, and generationally diverse) grapples with endless versions of the same dilemma. The episodes have all the ritual predictability of Japanese Noh theater [a very systematized genre]: Crimes are solved, lessons are learned, order is restored.

Reality TV presents some of the most vital political debate in America, particularly about class and race.

Reality shows have leaped into this imaginative void. Discovery's *Deadliest Catch*, which began its third season in April [2007], is an oddly transfixing series about . . . crab fishermen in the Bering Sea. As a straightforward documentary, *Catch* would have been worthy fodder, but the producers have made it riveting by formatting the whole season as a sporting event, with crab tallies for each of the half dozen or so boats and a race-against-the-clock urgency that, for all its contrivance, gives structure and meaning to the fishermen's efforts.

Exploring Real Issues

Narrative vibrancy is not the only thing that electrifies these shows. Reality TV presents some of the most vital political debate in America, particularly about class and race. Fox's *Nanny 911* and ABC's *Supernanny* each offer object lessons on the hazards of parenting in an age of instant gratification and endless digital diversion. ABC's *Extreme Makeover: Home Edition* features intensely emotional tales of people who have fallen through the cracks of [President George W.] Bush-era America—often blue-collar families ravaged by disease, healthcare costs, insurance loopholes, layoffs, and so forth. My channel's *The (White) Rapper Show* turned into a running debate among the aspiring white MCs over cultural authenticity—whether it is more properly bestowed by class or race.

Class realities are plumbed to remarkable effect on *The Real Housewives of Orange County*, a "docu soap" that completed its second season on Bravo this spring. The show is inspired by a trio of suburban dramas: *The O.C., Desperate Housewives,* and the 1999 movie *American Beauty.* Lacking the visual panache, or the budgets, of its scripted forebears, *Real Housewives* nonetheless goes deeper, charting the spiritual decay of life in gated communities, where financial anxieties, fraying families, and fear of aging leave inhabitants grasping for meaning and happiness as they steer their [Cadillac] Escalades across Southern California's perfectly buffed, featureless landscape. *Crash,* the 2006 Oscar winner, trafficked in similar white California dread, but with all the nuance of a two-by-four to the face.

In *Real Housewives,* businessman Lou Knickerbocker stages a photo shoot to promote his new "highly oxygenated" water, variously called "Aqua Air" and "O.C. Energy Drink" ("We have patented technology that produces water from air"). The models are attractive-ish teen and 20-something girls: Lou's daughter Lindsey, by ex-wife Tammy; a few other daughters of O.C. housewives; and a newcomer whom Lou apparently found waitressing at a local restaurant.

Lou and Tammy made piles of money—it's not clear how—but their finances seem to have fractured along with their marriage. The photo shoot, therefore, is throwing off more than the normal amount of flop sweat. Lou apparently has personally selected the girls, which means he has declined to showcase his other daughter, Megan, because of her tattoos and lack of physical fitness. Lou believes the "Aqua Air Angels" should embody the Aqua Air ideal, which is why they can't drink or smoke and must have grade-point averages higher than 3.5. "This is a photo shoot," he barks after a fight breaks out between one of the girls and the waitress, "not a gang bang, for chrissakes."

The best moments found on reality TV are unscriptable, or beyond the grasp of most scriptwriters.

The detail is what puts the scene over: Lou's lip-smacking focus on the girls, the girls' bland acquiescence. "That's it, baby, smile," Lou urges his daughter. "Show those teeth," says Tammy. A similar scenario on *Desperate Housewives* could never have been quite this preposterous, quite this blandly amoral. The characters would have been scripted with softening, redeeming qualities, or been rendered comically evil. Lou would've gotten his comeuppance, like [actor] Wallace Shawn's money-siphoning literary agent in that series. Here, the apparent willingness of the young women and at least some of the parents to indulge Lou's bottom-of-the-barrel scheming outlines, in a few short brushstrokes, a community's shared value system.

Emotional Truths Revealed

Value systems are smashed into each other, like atoms in an accelerator, on ABC's *Wife Swap*, where the producers find the most extreme pairings possible: lesbian mommies with bigots, godless cosmopolites with Bible thumpers. On one February show, a Pentacostal family, the Hoovers, was paired with the family of a former pastor, Tony Meeks, who has turned from God to follow his rock-and-roll dreams (mom Tish rocks out as well). "I feel by being there," Kristin Hoover said, "I was able to remind Tony that God still loves him and is not finished with him." The episode took seriously the Hoovers' commitment to homeschooling and their rejection of contemporary culture (a rejection not taken to the extreme of declining an invitation to appear on reality TV). Compare this with the tokenism of "born-again Christian" Harriet Hayes on NBC's dramedy *Studio 60 on the Sunset Strip*. Harriet's but a cipher, a rhetorical backboard against which ex-boyfriend Matt Albie can thwack his heathen wisecracks.

The resistance to reality TV ultimately comes down to snobbery, usually of the generational variety.

The competitions and elimination shows are latter-day Milgram experiments [psychological experiment in which subjects were told to administer electric shocks to test-takers] that place real people in artificial situations to *see what happens*. *The Apprentice* is Darwinism set loose inside an entrepreneurial Habitrail [a maze-like hamster cage]. Post-9/11, *Survivor* became less a fantasy and more a metaphor for an imagined postapocalyptic future. What happens on these shows might be a Technicolor version of how we behave in real life, but so is most fiction. Creative endeavors—written, scripted, or produced—should be measured not by how literally they replicate actual life but by how effectively they render emotional truths. The best moments found on reality TV are unscriptable, or beyond the grasp of most scriptwriters. It's no coincidence that 2006's best scripted dramas—*The Wire*, HBO's multi-season epic of inner-city Baltimore; and *Children of Men*, Alfonso Cuarón's futuristic thriller—were studies in meticulously crafted "realness," deploying naturalistic dialogue, decentered and chaotic action, stutter-step pacing, and a reporter's eye for the telling detail. *The Wire*'s season and Cuarón's movie both ended on semi-resolved novelistic notes, scorning the tendency in current television and cinema toward easy narrative closure. Watching them only threw into higher relief the inability of so much other scripted product to get beyond stock characterizations and pat narrative.

Documentary Filmmaking Benefits

For all the snobbism in the doc community, reality TV has actually contributed to the recent boom in documentary filmmaking. The most successful docs of recent vintage have broken through in part by drawing heavily from reality television's bag of tricks, dropping the form's canonical insistence on pure observation. In *Fahrenheit 9/11*, Michael Moore brings an Army recruiter with him to confront legislators and urge them to enlist their children in the Iraq War effort. In *Bowling for Columbine*, Moore takes children who were shot at Columbine to a Kmart, where they ask for a refund on the bullets that are still lodged in their bodies. Of course, Moore's never been a doc purist. *TV Nation*, his short-lived 1994 television series, prefigured a long line of gonzo reality, from *Joe Millionaire* to *Punk'd*. Having the Serbian ambassador sing along to the Barney theme song ("I love you, you love me") while statistics about the number of Bosnians killed during the breakup of Yugoslavia appeared on the screen was not only ur-reality; it was ur-Borat [the comedic title character of the 2006 hit mock-umentary *Borat*]. And speaking of talking animals, *March of the Penguins* turned stunning footage of mating and migrating penguins into an utterly contrived Antarctic version of [the 1970 romantic drama] *Love Story*.

The resistance to reality TV ultimately comes down to snobbery, usually of the generational variety. People under 30, in my experience, tend to embrace this programming; they're happy to be entertained, never mind the purity of conception. As an unapologetic producer of reality shows, I'm obviously biased, but I also know that any genre that provokes such howls of protest is doing something interesting. Try the crab.

2

Reality TV Has Lowered Standards for Television and Society as a Whole

James Wolcott

James Wolcott is a journalist and author, best known as a culture critic for Vanity Fair *and the* New Yorker. *He has published a novel titled* The Catsitters *and an autobiography,* Lucking Out: My Life Getting Down and Semi-Dirty in Seventies New York.

Reality television's cost-cutting and low production standards have eroded the quality of all network programming, scripted or unscripted. Furthermore, the genre's need to sensationalize meaningless conflict and celebrate antisocial conduct has created a generation of vacuous, self-centered viewers whose only aspiration is to appear on television.

I was recently in a Duane Reade drugstore, having a Hamlet fit of temporizing over which moisturizer to choose, when the normal tedium pervading the aisles was suddenly rent by the ranting distress of a young woman in her early 20s, pacing around and fuming into her cell phone. She made no effort to muffle her foulmouthed monologue, treating everyone to a one-sided tale of backstabbing betrayal—"She pretended to be my friend and shit all over me"—as mascara ran down her cheeks like raccoon tears. Judging from the unanimous round of stony expressions from customers and cashiers alike, her *cri de coeur* ["cry from the heart"] engendered no sympathy from the jury pool, partly because there was something phony about her angst, something "performative," as they say in cultural studies. Her meltdown was reminding me of something, and then it flashed: this is how drama queens behave on Reality TV—a perfect mimicry of every spoiled snot licensed to pout on Bravo or VH1 or MTV. The thin-skinned, martyred pride, the petulant, self-centered psychodrama—she was playing the scene as if a camera crew were present, recording her wailing solo for the highlight reel. Proof, perhaps, that the ruinous effects of Reality TV have reached street level and invaded the behavioral bloodstream, goading attention junkies to act as if we're all extras in their vanity production. There was a time when idealistic folksingers such as myself believed that Reality TV was a programming vogue that would peak and recede, leaving only its hardiest show-offs. Instead, it has metastasized like toxic mold, filling every nook and opening new crannies. *Idiocracy*, Mike Judge's satire about a future society too dumb to wipe itself, now looks like a prescient documentary.

There's no question that reality programs often resemble drama workshops for hapless amateurs.

I'm not talking about competition shows where actual talent undergoes stress tests as creative imagination and problem solving enter a field of play—elimination contests such as *Project Runway*, *Top Chef*, and, for all its sob-sisterhood, *America's Next Top Model*. It's the series that clog the neural pathways of pop culture with the contrived antics of glorified nobodies and semi-cherished has-beens that may help pave the yellow brick road for Sarah Palin, *Idiocracy*'s warrior queen. It is a genre that has foisted upon us Dog the Bounty Hunter, with his racist mouth and Rapunzel mullet; tricked-out posses of *Dynasty*-throwback vamps and nail-salon addicts (*The Real Housewives of Atlanta*, et al., the stars of which pose in the promos in tight skirts and twin-torpedo tops like lamppost hookers auditioning for *Irma la Douce*); and endless replays of Rodney King throwing up on *Celebrity Rehab with Dr. Drew*. The influence of Reality TV has been insidious, pervasive. It has ruined television, and by ruining television it has ruined America. Maybe America was already ruined, but if so, it's now even more ruined. Let us itemize the crop damage.

What kind of "acting" do we get from Reality TV? Eyerollings. Dirty looks. Stick-figure Tinkertoy gestures. Incensed-mama head-waggings. Jaws dropped like drawbridges to convey stunned indignation.

Reality TV Has Lowered Network Property Values

On his weekly blog, author James Howard Kunstler (*The Long Emergency*) noted the significance of a memorial tribute to CBS news giant Walter Cronkite on *60 Minutes* being followed by "a childish and stupid 'reality' show called 'Big Brother,'" an Orwell-for-dummies exercise set in a hamster cage for preening narcissists where cameras surveil every calculated move. Kunstler observed, "This [scheduling] said even more about the craven quality of the people currently running CBS. It was also a useful lesson in the diminishing returns of technology as applied to television, since it should now be obvious that the expansion of cable broadcasting since the heyday of the 'big three' networks has led only to the mass replication of video garbage rather than a banquet of culture, as first touted." Not entirely so. Quality cable dramas such as *Nurse Jackie, The Wire, The Shield, Deadwood, The Sopranos, Breaking Bad*, and *Mad Men* have immeasurably enriched our petty lives, though there's really no excuse for *Californication*. But it is also true that the mega-dosage of reality programming has lowered the lowest common denominator to pre-literacy. Cable networks originally conceived as cultural alcoves, such as Bravo and A&E (Arts and Entertainment), abandoned any arty aspirations years ago and rebranded themselves as vanity mirrors for the upwardly mobile (Bravo) and police blotters for crime buffs (A&E). Pop music has been all but relegated to the remainder bin at MTV and VH1, where high-maintenance concoctions such as Paris Hilton, Flavor Flav, and Hulk Hogan's biohazard clan of bleached specimens provide endless hours of death-hastening diversion. Since reality programming is cheaper to produce than sitcoms or ensemble dramas (especially those requiring location shooting, which is why the *Law & Order* franchises spend less time on the streets, more time haunting the shadows of dimly lit sets), intricate brainteasers such as *Bones* (Fox), *Lost* (ABC), and the original *CSI* (CBS) have to fight even harder to hold their own against the plethora of reality shows catering to romantic fools looking to land a rich sucker—all those Bachelors and Bachelorettes sniffing red roses between tongue-wrestlings.

Reality TV Has Annihilated the Classic Documentary

When was the last time you saw a prime-time documentary devoted to a serious subject worthy of [legendary broadcast journalist] Edward R. Murrow's smoke rings? Since never, that's when. They're extinct, relics of the prehistoric past, back when television pretended to espouse civic ideals. Murrow and his disciples have been supplanted by Jeff Probst, the grinny host of CBS's *Survivor*, framed by torchlight in some godforsaken place and addressing an assembly of coconuts.

While the queen bee of Reality TV, Bravo executive Lauren Zalaznick, is fawned over in a *New York Times Magazine* profile by Susan Dominus that elevates her into the Miranda Priestly [a character from the 2006 film *The Devil Wears Prada*] of the exegetical empyrean ("To her, what she's producing isn't rampant consumerism on display to be emulated or mocked, or both—it's a form of social anthropology, a cultural text as worthy of analysis as any other, an art form suitable for her intellect"), temporary serfdom is the lot of the peon drones being pushed to the breaking point. In an eye-opener published in *The New York Times* of August 2, reporter Edward Wyatt revealed the sweatshop secrets of Reality TV's mini-stockades, where economic exploitation and psychological manipulation put the vise squeeze on contestants. "With no union representation, participants on reality series are not covered by Hollywood workplace rules governing meal breaks, minimum time off between shoots or even minimum wages," Wyatt wrote. "Most of them, in fact, receive little to no pay for their work." The migrant camera fodder is often kept isolated, sleep-deprived, and alcoholically louche to render the subjects edgy and pliant and susceptible to fits. "If you combine no sleep with alcohol and no food, emotions are going to run high and people are going to be acting crazy," a former contestant on ABC's *The Bachelor* said. And crazy makes for good TV, whether it's [actor] Jeff Conaway unhinging on *Celebrity Rehab with Dr. Drew* ("911!") or some Bridezilla losing her precious shit over a typo in the wedding invitation. One particularly awful Bridezilla, named Karee Gibson Hart, whose threatening antics may have violated her probation, defended herself by claiming she was simply "playing the game," putting on a diva act to show off her dramatic skills. Judge Judy might not buy that excuse, but there's no question that reality programs often resemble drama workshops for hapless amateurs, a charmless edition of *Waiting for Guffman* [1996 comedy about amateur actors with dreams of Broadway].

Reality TV Has Debased the Time-Honored Art of Bad Acting

Bad acting comes in many bags, various odors. It can be performed by cardboard refugees from an Ed Wood [director legendary for low quality films] movie, reciting their dialogue off an eye chart, or by hopped-up pros looking to punch a hole through the fourth wall from pure ballistic force of personality, like [actor] Joe Pesci in a bad mood. I can respect bad acting that owns its own style. What I can't respect is bad acting that doesn't make an effort. In [pop artist] Andy Warhol's purgatorial version of home movies, those clinical studies of dermatology in action, his casts of beefcake/speed-freak/drag-queen exhibitionists had to work it for the camera, which kept rolling whether the objects of inspection were re-applying an eyelash or hogging the bathtub; his superstars had volumes of dead air to fill, no matter how near they were to nodding out. In [director] John Cassavetes's cinéma vérité [a highly stylized documentary style] psychodramas, the actors were hot-wired for improvisation, encouraged to trust their ids and forage for raw truth stashed beneath the polite lies that make up our sham existence. These lancings of bourgeois convention weren't pretty, but they required sustained outbursts from the showboats involved, an expansive temperament. What kind of "acting" do we get from Reality TV? Eye-rollings. Dirty looks. Stick-figure Tinkertoy gestures. Incensed-mama head-waggings. Jaws dropped like drawbridges to convey stunned indignation.

Reality TV Thrives on Envy and Spite

Nearly everyone conforms to crude, cartoon stereotype (bitch, gold digger, flamboyant gay, recovering addict, sofa spud, anal perfectionist, rageaholic), making as many pinched faces as the Botox will permit, a small-caliber barrage of reaction shots that can be cut from any random stretch of footage and pasted in later to punctuate an exchange. (Someone says something unconstructive—"That outfit makes her look like a load"—and *ping*! comes the reaction shot, indicating the poison dart has struck home.) Younger reality stars may have more mobile faces, though in time they too will acquire the Noh masks of the celebrity undead. Their range of verbal expression runs mostly from chirpy to duh, as if their primpy little mouths were texting. The chatty, petty ricochet of Reality TV—the he-said-that-you-said-that-she-said-that-I-said-that-she-said-that-your-fat-ass-can-no-longer-fit-through-the-door—eventually provokes a contrived climax, a "shock ending" that is tipped off in promos for the show, teasers replayed so frequently that it's as if the TV screen had the hiccups. The explosive payoff to the escalating sniper fire on *The Real Housewives of New Jersey* was a raging tantrum by Teresa Giudice, who flipped over a restaurant table in a She-Hulk fit of wrathful fury and called co-star Danielle Staub a "prostitution whore" (an interesting redundancy), all of which helped make for a unique dining experience and quite a season finale. Good manners and decorum are anathema to Reality TV, where impulsivity swings for the fences.

In the voyeurism of Reality TV, the viewer's passivity is kept intact, pampered and massaged and force-fed Chicken McNuggets of carefully edited snippets that permit him or her to sit in easy judgment and feel superior at watching familiar strangers make fools of themselves.

Reality TV Encourages and Rewards Vulgar Behavior

Ever since "Puck" put MTV's *Real World* on the map with his nose-picking, homophobic, rebel-without-a-clue posturings and earned notoriety as the first contestant to be evicted from the premises, self-centered jerkhood has put reality's lab rats on the publicity fast track. On Bravo's *Shear Genius*, Tabatha Coffey, doing a sawed-off version of Cruella De Vil, gloated with nasty delight after being eliminated from the show in a team challenge, because she was able to take a despised rival down with her; she exuded such Schadenfreude that she made losing look like sweet victory, a sacrifice worth making to louse up someone else's chances. And what was the fallout from her unsporting, cold-dish behavior? Why, she received her own Bravo show—*Tabatha's Salon Takeover*, where she got to be a bossy boots, bestowing her bad attitude on the less fortunate. TLC's *Jon & Kate plus Eight* was a popular, wholesome family favorite, but it was a tacky act of alleged infidelity that turned the marital split of Jon and Kate Gosselin into a nova express, their uncivil war splashed across checkout-magazine covers as America took sides, choosing between Jon, the philandering dope with the dazed expression, and Kate, the castrator with the choppy Posh Spice hair. We are now stuck with them for the foreseeable future, just as we are saddled with MTV's *The Hills'* Spencer Pratt, who has just brought out a book—which is probably one more than he's ever actually read—in which he caddishly boasts about his bastardly behavior toward Lauren Conrad, exulting in the wet hisses he and his wife, Heidi Montag, receive as America's least-admired bobbleheads. From the New York *Daily News*: "He brags in the book that he made a point of telling every blog around that a sex tape of nemesis [and former *Hills* star] Lauren Conrad existed. Why? Because he could. He . . . says he wouldn't have personally attacked Conrad had she not been so darn nasty to his then-girlfriend Montag." He's now thumping his chest in triumph at having helped drive Conrad off the show. "'If I weren't me, I'd hate me,' he announces." I hate him and I've never even seen *The Hills*, which only testifies to Reality TV's phenomenal outreach, its ability to annoy even the uninitiated.

The ego maneuvers of a Tabatha or Spencer are minor-league Machiavelli [a fifteenth-century historian and philosopher known for his cynical theories on manipulation and political power] compared with the latest scar on Reality TV's record—the savage murder of former bikini model Jasmine Fiore, whose mutilated body was jammed into a trunk and discovered in a Dumpster. The chief suspect was her former husband, a reality star named Ryan Alexander Jenkins, whose paltry claim to fame was his having been a contestant on the VH1 reality show *Megan Wants a Millionaire*, that ample contribution to humanity. (The Megan in want of a millionaire is Megan Hauserman, a graduate of VH1's *Rock of Love: Charm School*, who aspires to the title of "trophy wife.") "The case cast an unsettling light on the casting practices of reality television, in particular the sometimes tawdry shows broadcast by VH1," reported Brian Stelter, in a *New York Times* story headlined, with a delicate understatement bordering on self-parody, KILLING RAISES NEW REALITY TV CONCERNS. Proper vetting would have revealed that Jenkins had been previously convicted of assault against a woman and would perhaps have disqualified him from appearing on *Megan Wants a Millionaire* and *I Love Money 3* (also VH1). Nine days after Fiore's disappearance, Jenkins was found hanging dead in a motel room, his suicide completing the circle of misery, brutality, and fame-grubbing futility. In his final caper novel, *Get Real*, the late Donald Westlake had his woebegone protagonist Dortmunder and his gang cast in a Reality TV series that would have them plotting and executing a heist as a camera crew tagged along, borderline accomplices in crime. An ingenious story line, but *Get Real* may have been outdone and then some by the Brazilian series *Canal Livre*, whose host, Wallace Souza, is alleged to have commissioned a fistful of murders to bump off rivals in the drug trade and to ensure that his cameras would be the first on the scene for the buzzard feast (arriving so promptly that gun smoke was still streaming from one victim's body). Ordering a hit and then dining out on the corpse—talk about controlling supply and demand at both ends!

Reality TV Gives Voyeurism a Dirty Name

For film directors from Alfred Hitchcock to Andy Warhol to Brian De Palma to Sam Peckinpah (whose last film, *The Osterman Weekend*, was set in a house rigged with closed-circuit TV) to Michael Haneke (*Caché*), voyeurism has been one of the great self-reflexive themes in postwar cinema, James Stewart with his zoom lens in *Rear Window* being the primary stand-in for us, the audience, spying at life through a long-range gaze. In thrillers, the idle viewer becomes implicated, ensnared, in the drama unfolding and discovers that voyeurism is a two-way mirror: Raymond Burr, the watched, glares across the courtyard and meets Stewart's binocular gaze—*contact*. In the voyeurism of Reality TV, the viewer's passivity is kept intact, pampered and massaged and force-fed Chicken McNuggets of carefully edited snippets that permit him or her to sit in easy judgment and feel superior at watching familiar strangers make fools of themselves. Reality TV looks in only one direction: down.

3

Producers Sometimes Distort Reality and Undermine the Value of Reality TV

Andy Dehnart

Andy Dehnart is a television critic and journalist whose work has appeared on National Public Radio and in publications such as Playboy, Wired, *and* Salon. *He is the proprietor of* Reality Blurred, *a blog devoted to reality television news and analysis, and is the director of the journalism program at Stetson University.*

The recent controversy over a participant on the HGTV reality show House Hunters *claiming that parts of the show are faked provides insight into the amount of trust that viewers place in reality TV producers and the frequency with which that trust is broken. Such manipulation is not really necessary to create interesting reality shows; viewers want to see real situations that have real consequences on participants' lives.*

The genre of reality TV is once again on trial after a home buyer featured on HGTV's *House Hunters* told her story in a blog post, asserting that the show is heavily staged and even deceptive. Fans of the series reacted with a mixture of disgust, apathy, and assurances that they knew all along but didn't care.

Meanwhile, two larger and extremely familiar arguments emerged: All reality TV is all fake, and it doesn't matter if it is fake.

Neither is true. Whether or not reality TV is real actually matters.

First, incorrectly claiming all reality television is fake is like writing off every memoir as a lie, or all documentaries as fiction. Sure, some memoirists have lied or stretched the truth, but to lump all of them together is absurd. Likewise, it's ridiculous to pretend all reality TV is alike, especially when there's a ridiculously diverse array of programming that falls under that umbrella. Some is so heavily staged that it's bizarre that the producers are going to so much trouble to convince us it's real. Some is so brutally honest and real it's painful to watch.

It's important to discuss, analyze, and consider the degrees of reality in our unscripted television, from the ridiculous to the raw, especially because that description has meaning.

A Contract with the Audience

Labeling a television show as "reality TV" represents a contract with the audience that the program has consequence to its real-life cast members. A network is saying to its potential viewers: This show will affect real people, whether they are people who are just like you or are fun for you to mock. Whether cast members are competing for $1 million or just being filmed in their daily lives, their experience in front of cameras has an actual impact on them.

Reality-show cast members can lose their jobs or get mobbed by morons on Twitter and Facebook. Or they can become wealthy and famous, building off of their success and popularity. What we watch of reality cast members on television can be ridiculous and trivial, or the consequences can be life or death: Two years ago [2010], Discovery's *Deadliest Catch* chronicled the death of one of its captains in an emotionally powerful and exceptionally artistic way.

The bottom line is simple: The people on our screens can be affected, and *we* can be affected by them. That contract, that promise of consequence and authenticity, is what causes people to tune in, to tweet about the show, and to generate ratings and advertising dollars.

From concept to final edit, there are hundreds— thousands, even—of choices that have to be made that affect how closely the final product matches reality.

As engaged and moved as we can be by the characters in *Mad Men, Game of Thrones, Girls,* or *Parks & Recreation,* we know their characters aren't real. The actors aren't in jeopardy. They're people who make headlines and usually go on to other projects. They are not at risk of being killed, as are the people featured on—and people who film—Animal Planet's *Whale Wars,* for example.

Crafting Reality

Those real people whose lives and experiences are taped do share one thing with actors: they have teams of people working behind the scenes to turn footage of them into something watchable. To tell true-life stories as narrative, often serialized entertainment, a significant amount of craft is involved. Just filming someone 24/7 isn't entertainment; watch the *Big Brother* live feeds on Showtime for definitive proof of that.

The degree of reality is affected by that process. From concept to final edit, there are hundreds—thousands, even—of choices that have to be made that affect how closely the final product matches reality. People have to be cast, story producers have to find narratives in raw footage, time has to be compressed. Only the most compelling footage and dialogue will survive. Even the best documentary film is heavily crafted—

manipulated?—with footage carefully selected and ordered to make the best story or argument possible.

The problem comes when this process changes the reality of the situation, whether that manipulation is happening in real time—producers coaching cast members, reshooting scenes over and over again—or occurs during editing. To observe the heavy hand of producers and networks at work, watch an episode of the U.K. version of *Ramsay's Kitchen Nightmares* followed by an episode of the Fox adaptation, *Kitchen Nightmares*. Both capture a reality: Gordon Ramsay helping troubled restaurant owners, yelling at them, and fixing their problems. But on the Fox edition, Ramsay works much harder to create conflict, and so do the editors; the show's credits note that footage may appear out of order, and that's often used to construct reactions or moments that may never have occurred.

The pointlessness of the fakery is what's really appalling.

When viewers are lied to about what really happened when a reality-TV show was filmed, the contract is broken.

Unnecessary Manipulation

The pointlessness of the fakery is what's really appalling. First, many networks and producers have shown that real people having genuine reactions and interactions in either real or artificial contexts can make for compelling television: A&E's *Intervention* and *Hoarders*, CBS' *Survivor*, *Whale Wars*, *Deadliest Catch*, Oxygen's *The Glee Project*, Bravo's *Top Chef*, Food Network's *Chopped*, HBO's *24/7*, History's *Top Shot*, to name just a few. All of those shows must massage reality to make their reality into TV shows, but they stay close to the truth of the experience.

HGTV implausibly defended *House Hunters'* deception with a detailed and non-defensive statement that argued time constraints led producers to "go back and revisit some of the homes that the family has already seen and we capture their authentic reactions."

Let's ignore for a moment the egregious breach of trust that comes from producers of the series sometimes using homes that were never considered by the buyer or, worse, aren't even for sale. HGTV's argument makes sense: it's hard to make a show about a home-buying decision in real-time because that process is so drawn out. Instead of using deception, *House Hunters* could easily take us through a buyer's thought process after the process concludes: We bought this house, but were considering these, and here's why.

That might be a less compelling narrative. But it also wouldn't require ordinary people who aren't actors to fake their reactions. And it wouldn't have resulted in a backlash because the truth would have been both on screen and in real life. There are modifications that result in fiction, and those that do not: The fact that *Survivor* uses stand-ins for helicopter shots of contestants during challenges doesn't change the outcome of the challenge filmed days earlier, it just gives us aerial perspective that wouldn't be possible during the actual challenge (that's why you never hear a helicopter hovering overhead).

That seems significantly different than, say, *Iron Chef America*'s various deceptions, such as telling its contenders three possibilities for the secret ingredient, allowing the chefs to practice long before the actual battle.

It's been 20 years since *The Real World* made its debut on MTV and 12 since CBS broadcast *Survivor*, which turned reality television into a phenomenon. Perhaps it's time we stop with the reactive, overly simplistic arguments people made in 1992, and start having real conversations about how our reality entertainment is constructed and what that means.

4

Attention-Seeking Participants Create Hollow Reality Characters

Jonathan Murray

Jonathan Murray is a television producer who co-created MTV's Real World, *widely considered the first modern reality TV show. He has since created or produced a number of successful reality shows, including* Road Rules, Project Runway, *and* Keeping Up with the Kardashians. *He and his production partner, Mary-Ellis Bunim, were inducted into the Academy of Television Arts & Sciences Hall of Fame in March 2012.*

The proliferation of reality television since the premiere of Real World *in 1992 has resulted in a wave of programs featuring participants seeking to emulate popular cast members or personalities from previous shows. This lack of participant authenticity is responsible for the attention-seeking behavior often blamed on reality TV.*

When I heard about the Colorado family and their runaway helium balloon last month [October, 2009], I took a deep breath. Richard and Mayumi Heene, in search of television fame, had apparently filed a false report that their 6-year-old son was alone and in danger in the balloon. I knew that wasn't going to be good for anyone—not the kid, not the family and certainly not the reality television genre, the field I helped create 20 years ago.

Reality television did not invent hoaxes. Before shows like *Wife Swap*, where the Heenes may have gotten their taste for life in front of the camera, dishonest people concocted tricks to sell stories to magazines and books to publishers. What was different this time was the apparent calculating attempt to use a child as a pawn to play the media and reality television for monetary gain.

It wasn't always like this. When my late partner Mary-Ellis Bunim, a producer of daytime soaps, and I came together in the late 1980s to create MTV's *The Real World*, reality television, as we know it today, was nonexistent. Our plan at first had been to do a scripted series about young people starting out their lives in New York. But a scripted show was prohibitively expensive, so we took the documentary approach instead. We quickly realized that an unscripted, real-life show would be much more relevant to MTV's young audience.

When Reality TV Was Real

Our model for *The Real World* was the 1973 PBS documentary *An American Family*, which turned a year in the life of a Santa Barbara, Calif., family into compelling television that captured real people's lives. In 1992, we put seven diverse young people together in a loft in New York City to, as the series's now-famous introduction promises, "find out what happens when people stop being polite and start getting real."

Julie Oliver, from Birmingham, Ala., was one of them. She wanted a chance to get away from her overprotective father, live in New York and pursue a career in dance. Her roommates were three singers, a model, a painter and a writer. All of them were in New York because it was the place to go to make their dreams come true; being on television was secondary. None of them saw it as a way to get rich.

In later seasons, some cast members sought spots on the show to shed light on issues they cared about deeply. Pedro Zamora, an HIV-positive man, used the show in 1994 as a vehicle to educate young people about safe sex. More recently,

Ryan Conklin, an Iraq veteran, used the show to offer a window on the war that has left many of his friends dead or injured.

While *The Real World* chronicles something very real, it does it in a contrived way. Rather than find seven young people already living together, we cast the roommates for ethnic, gender and regional diversity, and the stories they bring with them. The fact that they are all attractive personalities doesn't hurt, either.

Our challenge is to cast people who can't help but be themselves. That's getting harder and harder as people become more knowledgeable about what makes a good reality show.

We also design and light the environment the roommates will be living in, making it a fantasy house; we don't need a dumpy apartment as part of the reality. When we came to Washington for our 23rd season, which begins airing in December [2009], we chose a beautiful, century-old house on S Street near Dupont Circle. We don't tell the cast what to say, but we do edit the episodes to contain stories with a beginning, middle and end.

When the show premiered in 1992, no one at MTV—or anywhere else—realized the impact the series would eventually have on television. It wasn't until 2000 that the broadcast networks embraced reality television with such shows as *Big Brother* and *Survivor*. For those networks, a reality soap such as *The Real World* doesn't guarantee explosive conflict and big ratings. They want reality television with a competition or format that ensures drama.

A People-Based Genre

No matter what's happening—a home being drastically remodeled or young housemates fighting—the key to a show's success is the same: casting. It's the strong personalities and divergent backgrounds of the cast that ensure conflict, and conflict is the primary requirement of a story, whether scripted or unscripted. The first season of any reality show is usually its best because the cast doesn't know what to expect; and as producers, we're not always sure, either. It's this spontaneity that has the cast living in the moment rather than trying to play a role.

Our challenge is to cast people who can't help but be themselves. That's getting harder and harder as people become more knowledgeable about what makes a good reality show. One young woman told us in a casting interview that she'd be the "biggest bitch" the show had ever seen. What she and others like her don't realize is that we're looking for complex and nuanced people who haven't completely figured themselves out. We go to extremes during the casting process to avoid people who have applied to be on other reality shows or play the reality TV game like the Heenes may have.

Our job . . . is to ask enough questions to be confident that we're not being taken in by someone who wants an easy route to money and fame.

We're not looking to cast perfect people, but we do want honest people. We thought very carefully about what we were doing when we brought cameras into that New York loft in 1992. We wanted to capture that messy time in a young person's journey, when it's possible to try on different identities and make mistakes and be forgiven for them. The title of the show, *The Real World*, was chosen to reflect that unique time in life and to reinforce the documentary nature of the program. By staying true to our title, we aim to stay relevant.

Some will blame reality television for the Heene family's actions—and the lengths to which people will go for a small taste of fame. But that's not fair. Trickery in the name of gaining a little attention didn't start with television, and it certainly wouldn't end if we stopped every camera crew currently following someone around a house, on a date or on a deserted island.

Our job—whether we're reality producers, book publishers, magazine editors or cable news executives—is to ask enough questions to be confident that we're not being taken in by someone who wants an easy route to money and fame.

The genre is called "reality television" after all. It's supposed to be real.

5

How a "Real Housewives" Suicide Sheds Light on Exploitation in Reality TV

Stephen Galloway

Stephen Galloway is the executive editor of features at the Hollywood Reporter, *where he previously worked as a reporter and film editor. He has also been a contributor to the* Los Angeles Herald-Examiner *and* TV Guide.

The tragic suicide of Real Housewives of Beverly Hills *participant Russell Armstrong, who was vilified in the show's first season, should trigger increased scrutiny on the way in which reality TV producers exploit participants' personal pain and suffering in pursuit of higher ratings. Since most reality shows have high profit margins, the subjects of these shows should undergo psychological screening and be compensated for their contribution. In cases of addiction, depression, or other psychological issues, long-term treatment should be provided.*

"Relax! Open up and Breathe! Feel comfortable in the uncomfortable!" A bearded man stomps through a circle of nine hapless students in a run-down Manhattan studio, yelling at the top of his voice. This is Robert Galinsky, 46, a former special education teacher and public-speaking coach who has reinvented himself as principal of the New York Reality TV School and aims to transform his students into stars.

"We're going to turn up the heat," he adds. "I want your name and your secret—now!"

Galinsky has agreed to let *The Hollywood Reporter* [THR] visit his training studio as part of a months-long look at reality TV's expanding genre of programming based on personal problems and sicknesses. A burly demolition man swathed in furs declares he has never read a whole book. A diminutive trainer reveals she was once a professional basketball player. And then we hit pay dirt.

"My name is Kristen Taylor," a tall, flame-haired woman murmurs. "I was a call girl"—and she's also a transsexual and a pastor's daughter. Perfect for any show about the impact of the sex industry on young women. As she starts to tell us her eye-popping story in the third-person plural, Galinsky cuts in.

"Speak in the 'I'!" he shouts. "Eliminate 'you, me, they, us.' It's all about me!"

"All about me" has become the mantra of reality TV, even if it means opening up painful private lives to cameras and sacrificing family and friends—and even, perhaps, if it means someone might die.

[Russell Armstrong's] plight was the extreme end of a business dependent on people with deep flaws, clinical phobias and other psychological issues.

The already pushed-to-the-limits reality TV industry was rocked Aug. 15 [2011] by news that Russell Armstrong, 47, the oft-featured estranged husband of Bravo's *The Real Housewives of Beverly Hills* star Taylor Armstrong and father of three, had committed suicide in advance of the show's second-season premiere. Armstrong's personal battles with his wife were documented in detail on the show. When he hanged himself at a friend's house, he was said to have been struggling with financial problems as well as overall concerns about his negative portrayal on the show (though he, and all other reality participants, sign waivers for filming). He told *People* magazine in July, "This show has literally pushed us to the limit."

The series will now be re-edited, according to Bravo president Frances Berwick, and might have its Sept. 5 [2011] debut delayed. But the suicide has set off a media firestorm, especially following reports that Armstrong wasn't even paid to appear on the show. As Bravo executives debate whether to air programming that documents a man's descent to suicide, Armstrong's family and victims' rights advocates have slammed the network for moving forward with the show in light of the tragedy.

"I don't want to see one frame of my son on the show next season," Armstrong's mother, John Ann Hotchkiss, told *The New York Daily News*. "I've never sued anyone in my life, but they aren't going to walk all over me and the family."

Armstrong was hardly alone in finding the reality of reality TV even more brutal than it appears onscreen. In fact, his plight was the extreme end of a business dependent on people with deep flaws, clinical phobias and other psychological issues.

An entire season of an A&E hit like Hoarders *can cost less than a few episodes of AMC's* Mad Men *and generate ratings on par with that acclaimed drama.*

Since launching in the U.S. with *Survivor* in 2000, unscripted television has moved beyond the competitions and dating foibles that defined its youth. Increasingly, the popular shows (especially on cable) document weaknesses of the human condition. A woman featured recently on TLC's *My Strange Addiction* carried around her husband's ashes until she began eating them (and then was institutionalized). The child mothers of MTV's *16 and Pregnant* and *Teen Mom* regularly grace the covers of celebrity magazines. All of this is taking a psychological toll.

As one longtime reality star admits to *THR,* "It's kind of warped my mind."

But the more outrageous the behavior onscreen, the more people watch. The Aug. 17 [2011] episode of MTV's *Jersey Shore,* which featured castmember Deena Cortese dabbling in booze-fueled lesbianism, pulled in 7.8 million viewers, powered by the youthful audience advertisers desire. Cable executives, thirsty for cheap programming, know that an entire season of an A&E hit like *Hoarders* can cost less than a few episodes of AMC's *Mad Men* and generate ratings on par with that acclaimed drama.

When *The Real Housewives of Orange County* first aired in March 2006, before the financial crash, it was "aspirational," focusing on the opulent lives these women were leading. But as the franchise grew, that conceit became untenable with 9 percent unemployment, so along came *The Real Housewives* of Atlanta, which still featured women with $3,000 handbags but introduced nearly nonstop catfights.

For a time, *Atlanta* was Bravo's highest-rated *Housewives.* That the stars often suffer personal problems outside the show—several have been sued or forced into bankruptcy protection—has not derailed viewer interest. But now that someone has hanged himself, all bets might be off.

"This is the worst-case scenario for the reality TV business," says one executive who declined to be named. "It's a very public suicide of a guy who was made to look absolutely terrible on that show. This death is causing people to think hard about the kinds of people we make shows about and whether they are equipped psychologically to be television stars."

Money is part of the problem.

Many hopefuls, including those in Galinsky's class, believe landing a show will make them rich. Like Taylor, the former call girl. Will this boost her $30,000-a-year income? "Absolutely," she says, no doubt influenced by stories about plucked-from-obscurity stars like Bethenny Frankel, who parlayed her fame gained on *The Real Housewives of New York City* into a spirits business she sold with a partner for $120 million. Reality stars such as *Jersey Shore*'s Mike "The Situation" Sorrentino and Nicole "Snooki" Polizzi earn about $100,000 an episode. [Former governor of Alaska] Sarah Palin was paid some $250,000 an episode for TLC's short-lived *Sarah Palin's Alaska*. Taylor Armstrong and her co-stars will make $135,000 apiece for season two of *Housewives*. (Armstrong was paid about $5,000 an episode for the first season.)

[Producers of reality TV] are operating in an environment that remains unregulated and inadequately scrutinized.

But most reality shows have casting budgets as low as $10,000 to $20,000 a season unless celebrities are involved.

Even celebrities get paid less than one might think. The big names on ABC's *Dancing With the Stars* are guaranteed a flat sum in the low six figures, but they only make significant money if they hang in till the final episodes.

"The goal isn't winning that mirror-ball trophy," says Gersh agent Todd Christopher. "It's about sticking around to keep increasing your fees."

Which makes Russell Armstrong's financial problems all the more glaring. While it would be simplistic to claim that Bravo or *Real Housewives of Beverly Hills* producers Evolution Media were responsible for his death, they are operating in an environment that remains unregulated and inadequately scrutinized. On many shows, for instance, participants sign "360-degree deals," notes Hayden Meyer, a partner and head of alternative TV at agency APA. That means the production company can take a percentage of any income a performer earns from books, appearances and the like.

Unfettered by contracts with AFTRA, SAG and other guilds, most networks have the right to replay each episode as often as they wish or to "repackage" series to create new episodes, without paying participants extra cash.

"It's a buyer's market," Meyer laments.

A 29-page contract obtained by *THR* for VH1's *Saddle Ranch* (the first season of which aired from March to June [2011]) shows how little onscreen talent can earn. For the gaggle of young men and women who appeared on the show—about waiters and waitresses at Los Angeles' Saddle Ranch Chop House—the contract stipulated each would receive "an all-inclusive fee for the Pilot equal to Five Hundred Dollars." The fee would go up to $1,000 for further episodes then increase by 5 percent per subsequent season or "cycle."

It also required that, for "no additional compensation," participants would be available when and where the producer wished to help with promotion.

Think that's bad? A contract for MTV's *The Real World*, recently leaked to *The Village Voice*, ties up participants for reunion shows and warns them that they could contract AIDS or other sexually transmitted diseases. The payoff for assuming such risks? Fifteen minutes of fame and a hefty dose of regret.

After attending an open casting call for *Survivor* with 5,000 others in 2005, Billy Garcia, a heavy-metal lover, went through a marathon session of interviews, all unpaid.

"There was a long, long process," he says. "You go to a regional interview, then to the L.A. final 50, and from that they took the 20 who actually got to film." Garcia was sequestered for 12 days in Los Angeles during the finals for season two, earning a paltry $100-a-day honorarium.

In all, he made $15,000 for the show, which is broadcast in more than 60 countries, and in order to get this he had to give up his day job at Blockbuster. That's a fraction of what Mark Burnett makes as executive producer; even for a flop like the Palin show, insiders say he made about $200,000 an episode.

Cable shows like [The Surreal Life and Flavor of Love*] have budgets that would barely cover catering for a primetime scripted series.*

"The worst thing to be is a contestant—they usually don't get paid," admits Mark Cronin, executive producer of *The Surreal Life*. On the whole, "They may get a stipend, but they don't make a per-episode fee."

That's true no matter how much contestants abase themselves, as they did on the *Surreal* spinoff *Flavor of Love*: In one case, a contestant defecated on the floor. The reward for this public humiliation? "Dating Flavor Flav," says Cronin.

Cable shows like these have budgets that would barely cover catering for a primetime scripted series. While major reality programs such as *American Idol* and *The Amazing Race* cost considerably more—the latter at one point topped $2.2 million an episode—"on the low end, an episode can be as inexpensive as $35,000 for one of the lifestyle shows on HGTV," says Meyer.

The broadcast networks average $600,000 to $700,000 for a one-hour reality show, but cable networks generally pay less than half of that. The budgets for two reality programs obtained by *THR*—on condition that the programs not be named—reveal how little of a show's money goes to the people onscreen.

The budget for an hourlong show with a three-day shoot came in at $741,651. Principal cast? $1. One 30-minute pilot cost $386,431. Onscreen talent? Zero.

Sitting in his airy Hollywood office, surrounded by a collection of pop-culture dolls, Doron Ofir is one of the experts in hooking the talent that makes these shows work. He's a leading casting director of reality shows, but he's not getting rich either and bemoans the fact that he and his peers receive no profit participation in the shows they cast.

Growing up in New York, the son of Israeli immigrants and bullied at school for being gay and effeminate, he wanted to escape, so "I would cut school, take the train, walk the streets, and by the time I was 15 I was already in the club scene."

Soon, Ofir was running those clubs, building an invaluable Rolodex along the way. "I've been collecting lists of movers and shakers," he says. Ofir moved to Los Angeles, where his lists paid off big-time in the reality world. He'd already found contenders for *Survivor* and *Temptation Island*, then a friend who worked for SallyAnn Salsano's 495 Productions asked him to cast *Jersey Shore*.

Because of where he grew up, "I knew what a 'guido' was," says Ofir, referring to the show's Italian-American cast. And he knew where to find guidos, too. With his database of 350,000 names and recruiters he sent to the tri-state area, he selected about 250 serious contenders and boiled them down to 50. For their first season, none got paid—though they've made millions since.

The personality-disorder people are the ones that end up in reality shows, without exception.

Ofir never expresses doubt about whether it was right to put inexperienced characters like these in front of a camera or about the long-term consequences to their lives; they are among the lucky few who have hit it big financially.

But he notes that each member of the final group was extensively screened for "psychology and background, to make sure they have no felonies, make sure that by the time you deliver them to the network they are a sealed package. There is a written exam, the Minnesota Multiphasic Personality Inventory, 500 questions that track inconsistencies in a person."

That's a test another reality kingpin, therapist Dr. Drew Pinsky of VH1's *Celebrity Rehab With Dr. Drew*, scoffs at, arguing testing must be better and that reality shows should provide counseling before, during and well after shooting.

During a recent roundtable, he told *THR* that these tests are hopelessly inadequate. "Unfortunately, the personality-disorder people are the ones that end up in reality shows, without exception," said Pinsky. "The psychiatric, psychological screening really doesn't ask very sophisticated questions. . . . The thresholds are ridiculous. They are on the order of, 'Have you ever thought about suicide before?'"

That question might not even have been posed to *Housewives*' Russell Armstrong as such tests are rarely given to secondary characters whose lives intersect those of the principals.

Psychological screenings help absolve reality producers from legal liability. But they also impart peace of mind. Consider Brian Gibson, co-executive producer of TLC's *Freaky Eaters*. Likable and well-meaning, he sits in a Burbank editing room watching an episode being cut together about Nikki, 34 (her last name is withheld by the show), a large woman who has an obsession with corn starch, which she downs by the box load.

"People want to be helped," argues Gibson. "Our show is inherently about helping people."

That's a view often repeated by those who work in the reality-sickness genre. Still, it's hard not to recoil as Nikki gets out of a car, a white cloud hovering over her from the foodstuff she has been consuming, or to see how people like this will be helped by having their obsessive-compulsive behavior aired for all to see.

Like many reality shows, Gibson says his company, Shed Media, pays for on-site therapy—though he acknowledges that there is a limit to how long this continues after shooting ends.

"The only way this can be good and healthy for these people is if there's a lot of very expensive aftercare," says Pinsky—something hardly any of the low-budget sickness shows have the money to provide.

Even Gibson admits other production companies are less scrupulous than his. "Sometimes," he says, "if you put great material first, the people can fall by the wayside."

That was certainly the case with the British reality show *There's Something About Miriam*, whose six male contestants sued, delaying the airing of the first season in 2003, because they hadn't been informed that the woman they were pursuing was transsexual. They settled for an undisclosed payment.

There's a veritable slew of low-budget . . . addiction shows that have no medical, psychological or guild regulations.

But Nancy Dubuc, president and GM of History and Lifetime Networks and one of the original executives behind A&E's addiction-themed *Intervention*, says she and her fellow executives go to considerable trouble to ensure people are given treatment.

"We walk the talk," she says. "From the launch of *Intervention*, which I was part of, we have always looked on it not just as a show but as an initiative. Addiction is a very serious problem, and we go out into communities and try to do something about it."

Her parent company, AETN, has been active in setting up town hall meetings to discuss addiction, creating a partnership with the nonprofit organization Drug Free America and instituting its own recovery project. "We do a great deal to follow these people beyond the program," Dubuc says.

That's equally true of A&E's *Hoarders*.

"We are on the set up to 10 hours a day, working with them for two days," says clinical psychologist Robin Zasio, who also travels with a professional organizer. Once the five-day shoot is over, "We provide aftercare services, dependent on each individual person."

Treatment combines cognitive behavioral therapy with exposure and response-prevention techniques. "We search out therapists in their area," she adds—all paid for by A&E and lasting as long as eight months.

"The producers have incredible compassion for the hoarders," Zasio says. "If I even thought there was exploitation, I would not be doing it."

One of the most talked-about hoarders, known as Glen the rat man, whose house became filled with some 2,000 rodents, is still being cared for many months after the episode featuring him was shot, she notes (though the show's reps said he would not be interviewed for this article).

But is this true of others? There's a veritable slew of low-budget *Hoarders* imitations and other addiction shows that have no medical, psychological or guild regulations. They can pretty much film what they want, with the participants' agreement, regardless of the sort of consequences Bravo might have to face, just as VH1 did before it.

When Ryan Jenkins, a contestant on the VH1 competition *Megan Wants a Millionaire*, was sought by police for the gruesome murder of his wife, the network scrambled to deal with the fallout of its poor vetting. Stung by criticism for its tawdry "celeb-reality" TV programming, VH1 withdrew all material related to the show from its website and immediately canceled the show. Bravo has not yet done that.

Other shows, like the syndicated veteran *Cheaters*, have remained on the air for years—even following an onscreen stabbing.

It's a late Saturday night in early spring, and Detective Danny Gomez sits in his black Mercedes, parked on a shady lane in a suburb of Dallas, waiting for one of his targets to step out of a house where he has been visiting his mistress.

Gomez, a stocky, happy-go-lucky man in his early 40s, has been with *Cheaters*—following unfaithful partners at the request of their significant others—since the show's inception 12 years ago. Fresh out of the police force, with his own detective agency, Gomez had no idea the program would turn him into a local celebrity when its producer asked him to be one of the main detectives on the series.

He also had no idea its host, Joey Greco, would be stabbed (though not fatally) by an infuriated subject in 2003, a reminder that the Armstrong incident isn't isolated.

None of which bothers Gomez, who's convinced snooping on cheating spouses and partners is positive in the long run.

"It does them good," he says.

He admits his work may have had a negative effect on him. He caught his brother-in-law cheating once and has been cheated on himself. "That hurt," he says, turning quiet. "Now it's very hard for me to be in a relationship. I see wedding pictures, a time in your life when things were good, and look what happens." Still, he says he wouldn't mind being filmed himself. "I'd want people to see it."

As Hollywood continues to profit from the personal problems of reality TV stars, the industry is taking note of the downside.

Snooping hasn't made Gomez rich (unlike executive producer Bobby Goldstein, who has made millions from the show). He lives in a modest $1,000-a-month apartment and spends most of his time working.

It won't make the people who appear on *Cheaters* rich, either: Most aren't paid a penny when they're shown on TV, even though they have to sign contracts agreeing to have the material aired. Oddly, almost all say yes; those who don't usually consent if they're given a few hundred dollars—at most, up to $2,000, according to Goldstein.

In a few minutes, Gomez's suspect will step out of his mistress' house, kiss her—all filmed by Gomez's flip camera—and find himself the next subject to feed TV's insatiable appetite for reality. Who knows what effect it will have on him.

Psychologists can debate whether *Real Housewives* contributed to Armstrong's suicide or merely held a camera up to a man who was deteriorating anyway. But as Hollywood continues to profit from the personal problems of reality TV stars, the industry is taking note of the downside.

"The difficult thing is, you are dealing with real people's lives, which haven't been fully explored or discussed," says Kevin Burns, executive producer of the Playboy-themed *The Girls Next Door*. "I really worry for the people who have been train wrecks on TV."

6

Reality TV Helps Bring Diversity to Television

Greg Braxton

Greg Braxton is a veteran staff writer at the Los Angeles Times, *covering arts and entertainment. He frequently writes about the role of African Americans in the entertainment industry and has appeared on National Public Radio to discuss the lack of opportunities for black actors in television and film.*

Despite its reputation for exploitation, reality television's desire to offer compelling social experiments centered on interpersonal conflict and competing worldviews makes it one of the most diverse genres on TV. In comparison to scripted television, which rarely features actors of color in leading roles, reality television gives minorities a fair chance to express their views and to become viewer favorites.

The much-maligned world of reality television is winning praise these days for "keeping it real" in an unexpectedly relevant way—reflecting a more diverse America than its more highbrow cousins in scripted prime-time shows.

Despite decades of public pressure on the major networks to diversify, the lead characters in all but a few of prime-time scripted shows this season are still white—and usually young and affluent. In contrast, reality programs consistently feature a much broader range of people when it comes to race, age, class and sexual orientation.

For example, CBS' *The Amazing Race* includes an Asian American brother-and-sister team and two African American sisters in its 14th season, which premiered Sunday. Three African Americans are in the current cast of CBS' *Survivor*. Four African Americans and two Tongan Americans have been featured on the current season of NBC's *The Biggest Loser*.

By contrast, a report released last year by the National Assn. for the Advancement of Colored People, titled "Out of Focus—Out of Sync," accused the networks of perpetuating a view of the nation that recalls "America's segregated past." The 40-page report charged that non-whites are underrepresented in almost every aspect of the television industry—except for reality programming.

That's no accident, according to reality TV producers and creators.

"We're looking to create shows that everyday people can relate to, and for that you really need a true representation of the population," said Dave Broome, executive producer of NBC's *The Biggest Loser*.

Being involved in reality TV is not always an uplifting experience. . . . But at least unscripted television is an equal-opportunity offender.

"A couple of seasons ago, there was an over-the-top character who was white that we could have cast, but we sacrificed that for a Latino. That's how important that is."

Business Decisions

The culture mix is driven by more than just political correctness. Although reality shows aren't directly in the business of bringing racial and ethnic enlightenment to America, they are in business. For shows that thrive on conflict and drama, a collection of cast members from varied backgrounds often serves that goal. Unresolved issues surrounding race, class and sexual orientation can either quietly fuel tension on programs or generate outright emotional explosions.

"I don't believe the makers of unscripted programs are necessarily all pro-social," said Jonathan Murray of Bunim-Murray Productions, whose shows include MTV's reality veteran *The Real World*. "A lot of times it comes down to the fact that diversity just makes those shows better."

Reality programming may be a . . . transformational force in bringing greater diversity to television today.

Of course, being involved in reality TV is not always an uplifting experience. Participants are subject to humiliation on the air (and, occasionally, eternal infamy on YouTube). The more outrageous the show's concept, the more likely contestants are to be ridiculed or even scorned. But at least unscripted television is an equal-opportunity offender.

Though the issue of race is often secondary to unscripted series' story lines, it does at times directly fuel the drama. William "Mega" Collins, an outspoken African American houseguest on the first edition of CBS' *Big Brother*, was the first evicted from the show after he angrily confronted his predominantly white fellow participants about race. CBS' *Survivor* in 2006 sparked a furor when the series initially divided tribes along racial and ethnic lines.

Just as the military and professional sports—two arenas not heralded for their liberal thought—became the unlikely vessels for breaking racial barriers decades ago, reality programming may be a similarly transformational force in bringing greater diversity to television today.

Vic Bulluck, executive director of the NAACP's [National Association for the Advancement of Colored People] Hollywood office, noted: "The marketplace has changed, and the producers of reality shows are obviously more sensitive or conscious of that change than the producers of scripted shows. It really comes down to relevance."

Stealing the Spotlight

Minority contestants have often done well in competition shows, such as ABC's *Dancing With the Stars* and Fox's *Hell's Kitchen*. By winning week after week, these contestants in effect become some of the programs' leading characters.

Network executives say that comparing the two genres [of scripted and unscripted TV] is unfair and that scripted shows are governed by creative restrictions that don't apply to reality TV.

(Two notable exceptions in which a reality program has yet to spotlight a person of color are ABC's dating franchise shows *The Bachelor* and *The Bachelorette*. In 17 total seasons, neither show's main role has ever been filled with a person of color. ABC representatives say they are "exploring" the issue for upcoming seasons.)

That's seldom the case with scripted comedies and dramas. Though the major networks—ABC, CBS, Fox and NBC—have in recent years made noticeable strides in assembling multicultural casts in ensemble shows such as *Heroes, ER, Lost* and *Grey's Anatomy*, there are still only five network shows with a minority actor playing a clear central character: NBC's *Law & Order* (Anthony Anderson), ABC's *Ugly Betty* (America Ferrera), ABC's *Desperate Housewives* (Eva Longoria Parker), CBS' *The Unit* (Dennis Haysbert) and CBS' *CSI: Crime Scene Investigation* (Laurence Fishburne). (In the 15 midseason network scripted series, including Fox's *Dollhouse*, ABC's *In the Motherhood* and NBC's *Kings*, only a few have a person of color in a central role.)

Network executives say that comparing the two genres is unfair and that scripted shows are governed by creative restrictions that don't apply to reality TV.

"When you're casting for an unscripted show, it's a much bigger universe and a whole different talent base," said Nina Tassler, president of CBS Entertainment. "It's real people versus actors.

"The casting in unscripted shows informs the storytelling," she said. "That kind of show starts as an idea, but then the story is developed by the cast. A scripted show is the brainchild of a creator who has a very specific vision."

Still, critics like Kristal Brent Zook, author of *I See Black People: Interviews With African American Owners of Radio and Television*, argue that diversity behind the camera in scripted programming will increase it in front of it. "It all comes down to what goes on in the writing room," Zook said. "It's a reflection on their imagination, or lack thereof. It's going to remain this way until you bring in people with wider experience."

7

Reality TV Stereotypes Minority Groups

Brian Lowry

Brian Lowry is a columnist and a critic for Variety, *an online entertainment news source.*

Reality TV shows like The Jersey Shore *and* Flavor of Love *rely on stereotypes of minority groups for entertainment. Careful editing exaggerate these stereotypes and help producers create the story they want to tell. A major concern with such stereotyping of people is that an undereducated audience will end up forming opinions of races and nationalities based on the reality TV they watch.*

The outrage expressed by some Italian-Americans over MTV's "Jersey Shore" marks a late-in-coming epiphany about reality TV programs—namely, how many traffic in stereotypes that, in a scripted context, would result in the writers being crucified.

Reality has largely gotten a pass because it ostensibly reflects "reality"—overlooking how participants are depicted as "characters" in much the way fictional personalities are. Tellingly, a recent *Newsweek* column titled "Kings of Queens" that focused on dramedies like "Glee" and "Ugly Betty" in examining resurgent gay stereotyping gave short shrift to all the royalty conspicuously displayed at Bravo.

Ignoring reality's excesses, however, misses the artifice built into such fare. Not only can producers employ editing techniques to carefully craft the stories they want to tell, but they're provided plenty of choices by the wannabe famous, who surely understand by now that outlandish and exaggerated behavior usually pays off in maximum exposure.

The latest offense against a minority group arrives courtesy of VH1. "Let's Talk About Pep" and "Fantasia for Real" follow musical acts Sandra "Pepa" Denton and "American Idol" contestant Fantasia. They're not-so-subtly presented as an American-American sitcom block, approximating UPN's "Girlfriends" and a single-mom comedy, respectively.

In "Fantasia," the characters include the singer's 28-year-old brother, Teeny, a committed moocher who test-drives expensive cars and responds with horror at the suggestion he get a job. Certainly, few sitcom writers would dare construct a similar portrait of a shiftless black man circa 2010, yet he's seemingly designed to become the show's breakout player.

Less-educated audiences are also tuning in, and perhaps drawing unflattering conclusions based on narrow stereotypes.

Not all reality-TV stereotypes are equally negative, but they do squeeze into the sort of little boxes that have been rightfully ridiculed in the past.

Gays, for example, almost invariably possess an enviable knowledge of fashion, cooking and decorating—presuming the "Queer Eye" is inherently superior to its straight counterpart. Yet watch enough reality in this genre and you'll notice less-laudatory traits as well, among them a tendency to become hysterical under pressure (see Oxygen's "Addicted to Beauty") and relentless cattiness that regularly lurches into the snide.

Nevertheless, subsets of minority communities—in some instances no doubt amused by rough-hewn images of themselves—embrace such programs, which in today's fragmented marketplace can be enough to render them commercially viable.

A less-settling prospect is that less-educated audiences are also tuning in, and perhaps drawing unflattering conclusions based on narrow stereotypes.

Admittedly, unscripted TV has wallowed in such imagery for years, but the shift has evolved in subtle ways.

Programs like "Jerry Springer" and other daytime talk- and courtshows portray an underclass full of knuckle-dragging cretins, obligingly indulging in affairs and disputes that lead to heated arguments and fisticuffs—the better to be lectured by the hosts.

Even more than drama, reality TV relies on this kind of lazy shorthand, leading to a flat-screen world where blondes are airheads and minorities are too-often shown fleeing from the cops (the latest offender in the latter camp being "Steven Seagal Lawman," an A&E series set in a depressed part of Louisiana).

The difference is that daytime TV churned out an ever-changing array of characters, whereas series like "Flavor of Love" and "Jersey Shore" are more insidious. Key participants represent an ongoing franchise, as opposed to mere bystanders granted 15 minutes of exposure. As such, their excesses are serialized and in success, magnified.

Moreover, in instances where celebrities (fallen or pseudo) are involved, they can be directly invested in the shows as producers—adding to the incentive to hit their mark, as it were, and play a predetermined part.

As the Newsweek piece concluded, there's room for broadly drawn characters provided that's not all the audience sees: "It's not that gay men and women should pretend to be straight, or file down all their fabulously spiky edges. . . . The key is balance."

But if fleshed-out minority roles are sometimes scarce in the scripted realm, thanks to reality TV's hyperbolic habits, such roles remain virtually nonexistent in "reality." And whatever alibis they might offer, unscripted producers know precisely what messages they're sending—from the haughty salons of Beverly Hills and mean streets of Jefferson Parish to the beer-soaked beaches of the Jersey shore.

8

Reality TV Presents Rural Americans as Skilled and Serious Workers

Robert Lloyd

Robert Lloyd is a television critic for the Los Angeles Times. *He has also been a reviewer at* LA Weekly, *where he contributed articles on music and television.*

Reality shows featuring workers in out-of-the-way locations, while often decried for depicting rural Americans as rednecks or hillbillies, in fact present a positive image of men and women who are willing to risk their lives to perform meaningful jobs. When compared to other reality shows, which often celebrate the wealthy and unmotivated, these programs come closer to representing the reality of most Americans' lives.

Living in the farther reaches of basic cable are a growing number of television series about what might be called "ordinary people" at work in what most of us would consider extraordinary jobs. It is lazily tempting, though not quite right, to describe these shows as redneck or blue-collar or rural, but they are mostly set away from big cities in places that—apart from these shows—you don't often see on TV: Southern places and prairie places and backwoods places.

You can link their titles into a kind of poetical associative chain: *Ice Road Truckers, American Hoggers, Lady Hoggers, Ax Men, American Loggers, Swamp Loggers, Swamp Brothers,*

Swamp People, Swamp Wars—do you see a pattern emerging?—*Bear Swamp Recovery, Lizard Lick Towing, Black Gold, Gold Rush* (formerly *Gold Rush Alaska*), *Flying Wild Alaska, Deadliest Catch, Hillbilly Handfishin'* and the just-begun *Big Shrimpin'.* They make their home on networks such as Discovery, History, TruTV, A&E and Animal Planet.

Even National Geographic Channel has its corn-pone science show, *Rocket City Rednecks*, which debuted in September [2011]. It is a sort of *Mythbusters* with an Alabama accent, whose, "backwoods geniuses" make rocket fuel from moonshine whiskey and armor a truck with beer cans.

Cable TV likes to show people at work; it is an economical way to mount a series. There is built-in color there and, with a little help, drama: There is always something that needs to be done (in almost anybody's life) on too little money and with too little time. The series listed above are the muddier cousins of shows like *Cake Boss* and *DC Cupcakes*, and of the many "get rich by serving the rich" series so beloved by Bravo.

For all the hokum, these are shows about getting the job done.

It is part of their point, which is as often as not clothed as comedy, that the work they show is physically dangerous, because of the landscape and elements in which it is performed and/or because it involves things, machine or animal or human, that might kill you. In Discovery's Appalachia-set *Moonshiners*, premiering Tuesday [December 6, 2011], the stars (Tim the Moonshiner, Tickle the Sidekick, Popcorn the Legend, as a promo spot names them), would appear—appear—to be breaking the law, which is a whole other sort of risk-taking. (The network also has *Weed Wars*, about the medical marijuana business, beginning Thursday [December 1, 2011].)

Real People, Meaningful Work

Blue collars and rednecks aside, these series are not really about class. A little financial struggle is good for the narrative, nevertheless, and we're regularly reminded of the money an enterprise is liable to lose when this or that thing goes wrong, but by and large these are not people operating on the margins. Neither is politics, which can be an alienating force in entertainment television, part of the package.

But the work does matter, especially compared to the rest of television, where it is mostly just a decoration. For all the hokum, these are shows about getting the job done. Expertise and capability, which also power cooking and home improvement shows, is just plain attractive, whether it's knowing how to keep a big truck running in arctic weather or how to wrangle a large and deadly snake into a trash can—for its own good, I hasten to add. (Not all animals are as safe here: You do not want to be an alligator in *Swamp People*, about people who kill them; ditto a wild boar in *American Hoggers* or a catfish around the Hillbilly Handfishers. Their shows come with viewer advisories you ought to take seriously.)

It is probably enough to say that there will be some in the audience who will identify with these characters and others who regard them as interesting specimens. They speak in Cajun cadences, in the accents of Maine and Oklahoma. (Even MTV, which has just ordered *Buck Wild*, "following the colorful antics of a group of friends just out of high school in rural West Virginia," is looking in that direction.)

Some smoke cigarettes, and not to look sophisticated. They dress in their own clothes, for comfort or for work. Many could stand to lose a few pounds, to start. With some exceptions—the female characters tend to be conventionally hot, conventionally—they are not like people Hollywood casts for lead roles. Some are even old—the men of *Gold Rush*, out of work and prospecting for gold, are almost all in their 40s, 50s and 60s, and that is part of the story. As TV, there is something refreshing about it.

As with most reality TV, the reality in these series is modified and mediated. TruTV's motto, "Not reality, actuality," is a tacit admission that reality is now an empty word, although the network is home to the comically unconvincing repo shows *Bear Swamp Recovery* and *Lizard Lick Towing*, which pits its heroes against deadbeat strippers, prostitutes and moonshiners, as boss Ron Shirley delivers his colorful play-by-play. "She's madder than a hornet with no stinger, baby!" But as in professional wrestling, which this oddly resembles, the fakery is part of the fun.

9

Reality TV Shows Perpetuate Stereotypes about Southerners

Karen L. Cox

Karen L. Cox is an associate professor of history at the University of North Carolina at Charlotte. She has written a number of books and articles on southern history, including Dixie's Daughters: The United Daughters of the Confederacy and the Preservation of Confederate Culture *and* Dreaming of Dixie: How the South Was Created in American Popular Culture.

Reality TV shows based on southern culture do not present an accurate portrait of southerners or their lifestyle. These shows depict the South as either a mysterious and foreign region with a different heritage from the rest of the United States, or as a land of ignorant "good old boys" and daisy duke-wearing southern belles. In reality, southerners are far more diverse and educated than such portrayals would indicate, and these stereotypes only serve to discourage them from reaching their full potential.

If you go by the sheer number of programs and casting calls, reality television has become thoroughly Dixiefied. Whether it's Lifetime's *Glamour Belles*, truTV's *Lizard Lick Towing* or CMT's *Sweet Home Alabama*, series purporting to show a slice of Southern life are huge, and getting bigger: more than a dozen new programs have been introduced so far this year, while others have been renewed for second or even third seasons.

Such shows promise new insight into Southern culture, but what they really represent is a typecast South: a mythically rural, white, poorly educated and thickly accented region that has yet to join the 21st century. If you listen closely, you may even hear banjos.

These stereotypical depictions are insulting to those who live in the region and know that a more diverse South exists. Even worse, they deny the existence of a progressive South, or even progressive Southerners.

Southern reality TV programs fall into a few subcategories. Sometimes, producers seek to portray the South as culturally foreign to the rest of America, and they choose characters or remote locations that reinforce this image.

The History channel's *Swamp People*, for example, focuses on alligator-hunting season in southern Louisiana by showcasing individuals who live and work in the Atchafalaya Swamp, thereby preserving their "ancient way of life." The show uses subtitles to emphasize the cultural differences between the bayou and the rest of the country, even though the "stars" speak plain English.

We've been here before, with The Dukes of Hazzard *and* Green Acres—*and it's no surprise that more than one production company wants to take us back there.*

Other shows focus on those Southerners that Americans feel as if they already know, like Southern belles and hillbillies. In its own bid to buy into the trend, Animal Planet has given us *Hillbilly Handfishin'*, in which two Oklahomans, Skipper Bivins and his pal Trent Jackson, teach people, generally big-city Northerners, how to catch catfish by using their own limbs as bait.

Then there's *Sweet Home Alabama*, a Dixiefied version of *The Bachelorette*, only in this setting she is choosing between city slickers and Southern boys. It's not unlike the show with the catfish duo: both feature a competition between country and city or, put more pointedly, North and South. The message is reduced to a Hank Williams Jr. song: a country boy can survive.

Southern Stereotypes Are Nothing New

These stereotypes have a long history—we've been here before, with *The Dukes of Hazzard* and *Green Acres*—and it's no surprise that more than one production company wants to take us back there. Alongside *Hillbilly Handfishin'* is *Redneck Riviera*, a show still in development that trumpets itself as the Southern *Jersey Shore* and that has selected the racially insensitive Confederate battle flag for its logo.

The show is casting for type by seeking "guys and gals" who answer "yes" to the loaded question, "Do you drink sweet tea, talk endlessly about Nascar, sport a rebel flag (on your bikini or jacked-up pickup truck), listen to loud country and/or Southern rock, or enjoy walking around shirtless or in Daisy Dukes?"

There's no doubt that more than a few people would answer yes, especially when money and potential fame are involved. But millions of Southerners would say no—including the Indian communities of Mississippi, the Latinos who are now the largest minority in towns across the region and the thousands of white suburbanites who feel more of a connection with exurban Chicago or Denver than Lizard Lick, N.C.

In fact, the last decade has brought dramatic demographic changes to the region. The South's population is more ethnically and racially diverse than it ever has been. Hispanics are the fasting-growing ethnic group in the country and, according to census statistics, most of that growth has been concentrated in the South.

The region is increasingly urban and cosmopolitan, and has become more economically and politically powerful. Atlanta hosted the 1996 Summer Olympics, and Charlotte, N.C, will be home to the 2012 Democratic National Convention.

Therefore, you might expect better programming from the History channel. But don't hold your breath. It recently introduced the show *You Don't Know Dixie*, which promises to educate people about the South. But evidence to the contrary is right there in the opening credits: the term "Dixie" (instead of "South"), and the use of the Confederate battle flag to illustrate the "X," tell us the show is more concerned with simplistic mythmaking than piecing apart contemporary cultural complexities.

Indeed, the program is heavy on regional trivia and relies on "well-known Southerners" like [*Extreme Makeover* host] Ty Pennington and [comedian] Jeff Foxworthy (and a hillbilly moonshiner whose speech, like that of the folks on *Swamp People*, required subtitles) to tell us "hidden truths" about the region. These "truths" rarely involve women, and they reduce African-Americans to cooking and singing the blues.

It reinforces a message to Southerners themselves, particularly whites, that they are in fact benighted and backward—so why change?

And in *You Don't Know Dixie*, as in all these shows, "Southern" almost always means "white," regardless of the central role that blacks play in the region's culture.

It's not that other reality TV shows don't trade in stereotypes of other places, too—say, New Jersey or Los Angeles. But those shows never pretend to show the entirety of Jersey or Southern California life, just a cliched corner of it. Many of the Southern reality TV programs, on the other hand, trade in age-old stereotypes that indict the entire region.

Of course, one could ask why all the fuss about what is, ultimately, mindless entertainment? But there are two big problems. First, it gives non-Southerners license to point their fingers at a supposedly culturally deficient region, while ignoring their own shortcomings.

And second, it reinforces a message to Southerners themselves, particularly whites, that they are in fact benighted and backward—so why change?

To present the full scale of the South's diversity would do more than just undermine negative popular perceptions of the region. It would also ruin the stock in trade that has long been used by the dominant media to represent the South as a place that is culturally different from the rest of the country. Although of course, it wouldn't be as entertaining.

10

Reality TV Can Empower Women

Susannah Breslin

Susannah Breslin is an author and a blogger for Forbes.com who frequently writes on issues related to gender and sexuality. Her blog, The Reverse Cowgirl, *was named one of Time.com's twenty-five best blogs of 2008. She is the author of a book of short stories,* You're a Bad Man, Aren't You?, *and is a regular contributor to a number of print and online publications, including* Newsweek, Slate, *and* Variety.

Although reality television often depicts females as vapid and petty, women can learn lessons about ambition and self-confidence from even the most maligned programs. Female reality stars often exhibit characteristics that are valued in business settings, such as control, tenacity, and exuberance.

I'm one of those intelligent, educated women who has terrible taste in TV.

Hand me the remote, and I'll watch *The Real Housewives of Anywhere* for hours.

Mob Wives? Check. *Love & Hip Hop?* Check. *Jerseylicious?* Uh, check.

I don't know what's wrong with me that I feel compelled to endlessly immerse myself in the lives of women who commence catfighting at the drop of a weave, who throw each other under the bus on a regular basis, whose main claim to fame is their willingness to serve themselves up as a totemic feast for our consumption.

Lessons Learned

Of course, it's possible, albeit hard to believe, that reality TV, in fact, has something valuable to offer us—about work, at that.

TIP #1: Be the Alpha Dog. Reality TV's current lineup of stars features women who are alpha bitches. Think: *The Real Housewives of Atlanta*'s NeNe Leakes, *Kourtney and Kim Take New York*'s Kim Kardashian, *Tabatha Takes Over*'s Tabatha Coffey.

They may spend more time on their hair, applying lip gloss, and shouting at people than they do imparting actual words of advice, but what viewers learn by watching any of these women is that control is king. These are women who want the spotlight directed on them, who see the world and its population as things to dominate, who perceive the will of others as something to subjugate or ignore.

Kim decides she doesn't like her new husband, Kris Humphries. "I don't want to be married anymore," she announces, and that is the end of that.

Reality TV haters like to say the genre is an abomination, but maybe women enjoy its guilty pleasures because they don't feel like they're the CEOs of their own lives and on these shows females alpha dog their way to success.

TIP #2: Be a Fighter. If you look at all the ways women self-sabotage, you'll see a common thread. When women are put in situations where they are forced to fight for what they want, to *be big*, they shrink in response. They avoid confrontation, rather than embrace it. They think small, rather than thinking extra-large. They self-sabotage, rather than demand what they want.

Not so on reality TV. Any top reality TV performer knows catfights bring the viewers, and producers are more than happy for females to get scrappy.

Our fascination with reality TV catfights suggests we wish we had the balls to brawl more often than we do, to stand up for ourselves at home and at work.

On *Mob Wives*, Karen Gravano, the daughter of Sammy "the Bull" Gravano, pummeled Drita D'Avanzo at a party. Hair was pulled, an eye was blackened, and the event descended into chaos.

You can't jump your coworker or boss when they're driving you crazy, but our fascination with reality TV catfights suggests we wish we had the balls to brawl more often than we do, to stand up for ourselves at home and at work.

TIP #3: Be a Character. Don't want to do well at work? Let everyone else forget about you. "What do you do again?" If you get this question around the office, no one knows if you're indispensable or not.

On the latest season of *The Real Housewives of Atlanta*, NeNe Leakes enters every room as if the Queen has appeared to bless her subjects with her presence. An overpriced handbag dangling from one arm, teetering on sky-high heels, and almost always hiding behind over-sized sunglasses, Leakes is aware that she's a brand, not a person.

You may work for another company, but within that corporation, you're your own brand. What's your brand? How much is it worth? That's up for you to decide, and everyone else to believe.

11

Reality TV Intentionally Subverts Social Progress and Gender Equality

Jennifer L. Pozner

Jennifer L. Pozner is the founder and executive director of Women in Media & News, which advocates for female viewpoints in the media, and is the editor of the WTMN blog. She published a book-length study on gender, race, and class in reality television, Reality Bites Back: The Troubling Truth About Guilty Pleasure TV, *in 2010.*

Reality TV serves to counter social progress by placing women in roles that reinforce lingering gender stereotypes. Reality dating shows increasingly portray women as hopelessly dependent on men for support and validation, despite the fact that women are taking leadership roles in the highest levels of politics, academics, industry, and sports. This trend should be seen as a backlash against social progress and an attempt to undermine the feminist movement.

Step right up, folks, it's time for everyone's favorite guessing game, Regress-o-Rama. Who said the following?

"I will make the best wife for Bob because I will be a servant to him. And if he comes home from a long day at the office, I'll just rub his feet, and have dinner ready for him, and just [giggle] love on him!"

Was it:

Jennifer L. Pozner, "Reality TV (Re)Rewrites Gender Roles," *On The Issues*, Winter 2010. Copyright © 2010 by On The Issues. All rights reserved. Reproduced by permission.

A. Nicole Kidman as a subservient cyborg in the 2004 remake of *The Stepford Wives*

B. A devout attendee at the Southern Baptists' 1998 Convention, heeding her clergy's call for wives to "cheerfully submit" to their husbands

C. A single Mormon woman hoping to join the polygamous family in TLC's reality series, *Sister Wives*

D. Christine, a bubbly twenty-four-year-old administrative assistant on ABC's template-setting dating series *The Bachelor*, explaining why she should win a marriage proposal from some random dude instead of the 24 other hubby-hunting competitors he'd be making out with.

If you guessed "D," congratulations—you win! Christine said this during *The Bachelor*'s fourth season premier—before she'd ever met the man.

In the unscripted (but carefully crafted) world of dating, marriage and lifestyle shows, women are not concerned with politics, law, athletics, activism or even careers in general.

On second thought, we all lose.

Women and Reality TV

I began actively monitoring unscripted programming when *The Bachelor* debuted in 2002, sensing a new resurgence of a classic antifeminist media meme. Since then, reality television has emerged as America's most vivid example of pop cultural backlash against women's rights and social progress. Compare the accomplishments and experiences of American women over the past decade with their depictions through the unscripted looking glass, and a systemic pattern emerges.

The same year Condoleezza Rice became the first African American female national security adviser, in 2000, Fox aired the first major-network reality dating show, *Who Wants to*

Marry a Multi-Millionaire, a Miss America meets mail-order-bride parade based on the premise that women can only achieve success by proxy, as arm candy to rich men. In 2003, as female athletes scored new records in tennis, figure skating, soccer, swimming and pole vaulting, UPN unveiled *America's Next Top Model*, teaching young women that their bodies are valuable only as decorative props for advertisers—the skinnier and weaker the better. While military mom Cindy Sheehan was organizing mothers and families against war in 2004, ABC and Fox brought the news media's trumped up "mommy wars" to the boob tube in the form of *Wife Swap* and *Trading Spouses*, generally portraying women as bad wives and mothers if they pursued professional or political interests outside the home (and demonizing dads as wimps or poor role models if they were primary caregivers for their kids). By 2006 and 2007, when for the first time ever, women became Speaker of the House, president of Harvard, and commander of the International Space Station, yet on VH1's *Flavor of Love*, women—especially women of color—were depicted as ignorant, violent, gold-digging sluts, and TLC's *Say Yes to the Dress* presented thousands of dollars of name-brand beading and tulle as the key to female fulfillment. And in 2008, just as Hillary Clinton was campaigning for the Democratic presidential nomination and Sarah Palin became the GOP's first female VP candidate, Bravo's *The Real Housewives* franchise showcased women who aspire mostly to lives of leisure.

Nowhere has the backlash been more overt than in the reality relationship genre. American women have made great strides over the last decade in every professional field, and have redefined what love, family and happiness mean in the personal sphere. Yet in the unscripted (but carefully crafted) world of dating, marriage and lifestyle shows, women are not concerned with politics, law, athletics, activism or even careers in general (unless they're competing for the supermodel/starlet/rock star gigs that populate ten-year-olds' daydreams, or have schoolteacher/flight attendant/professional cheerleader jobs that were acceptable in the pre-feminist 1950s). Instead, reality TV producers, casting directors, editors and their product placement sponsors have collaborated to paint American women as romantically desperate, matrimonially obsessed and hypertraditionalist in their views about the "proper" role for wives and mothers, husbands and fathers.

Power imbalances in heterosexual relationships are codified in relationship shows.

Women Don't Lead on Reality TV

VH1 offers *Tough Love* via matchmaker Steve Ward, who opens every episode saying, "Nobody knows single women like I do. They're lonely. They're clueless. They're needy." Stylized illustrations of dapper dudes rejecting lovelorn ladies accompany this intro, rendering the Single American Female a symbol of misery. Through insults, paternalism and universal statements about "the male mind," Ward commands women to follow his "boot camp" rules or be alone forever. If he can't "train" these "slutty," "dumb," "soul-sucking" "losers," he barks, they'll never be able to land "Mr. Right."

Women who'd recoil at their presumed passivity or inferiority either are not cast, are edited to appear ditzy, or find their objections left on the cutting room floor. As a result, the "self-loathing single gal" (classic line: "I don't want to die alone!!!") joins the Bitch, the Bimbo, the Slut, and the Gold Digger as a dominant reality TV stock character. "I'm a loser . . . what is so wrong with me that someone cannot love me for who I am?" wept Heather in 2002 during a tear-stained money shot found in every Bachelor elimination ceremony. In a "where are they now?" series update, she discussed her only ambition: "My goal right now is to get married. You always hear those horror stories. You know, 'forty and single!'. . . I'm always nervous that Mr. Right is not going to come along." *Tough Love* was still playing by the same script in 2010, with sexy simpleton Liz confessing that when she's not "thinking about kittens or sunshine or something," she's feeling "like a failure" because she's "not married right now at twenty-four years old. . . . Walking down the aisle would finally make my life complete."

Power imbalances in heterosexual relationships are codified in relationship shows. *Tough Love* gives women ideological makeovers with advice ripped from 1950s finishing school manuals: "Act interested even though you're not." Laugh at men's jokes even if they're not funny. Don't be opinionated, do be "uncomplicated." On Bravo, *The Millionaire Matchmaker*'s Patti Stanger spells out gendered prescriptions point-blank: "It is so important for women to be women and men to be men, and to keep those roles intact. It's worked for millions of years." But what does that mean after 40 years of feminism? Simple, Stanger instructs: When you're on a date, "You listen. You're not the leader in this situation. You let the man lead. . . . You gotta, like, be the actress in the movie, not the director." Dating show hotties read from this script. "You can lead," a doe-eyed divorcée whispered while dancing with a Bachelor. "You can lead me in life. And that's what I want."

Despite how frivolous reality TV may seem or how much producers say it's all in good fun, the genre's psychological browbeating has political ramifications.

But what of men who want partners, not servants? *The Millionaire Matchmaker* shows them the error of their ways. When ex-NFL star Matt "Hatch" Hatchett said that he wanted a relationship with an "ambitious" "career woman," Stanger flipped out. Hatch "needs to shut his mouth," she told the cameras. "He wants it to be equal society here. . . . I'm really getting sick of this!" Far more typical was Jason, an overweight, seemingly stoned heir to the 20th Century Fox fortune, who wanted *The Millionaire Matchmaker* to locate his dream woman: "I want hot blond, big tits. Definitely funny. Kind of like a Stepford Wife." Potential Stepford wives are plentiful in the reality universe, so Stanger set him up with a girl who giggled when he "joked" that "You're the woman, you're supposed to serve."

Real Progress, Reality TV Backlash

Between 2000 and 2010, while reality producers focused on a narrow, regressive interpretation of marriage in which all single women are pathetic, all couples are straight, parenting and housecleaning are women's work, families can survive on only the income of a Strong Male Provider, and "love" is the sole domain of skinny white women and rich white men (not one person of color has headlined any of the 14 seasons of *The Bachelor* or six seasons of *The Bachelorette*), actual American couples were redefining relationships in countless ways. Women postponed marriage longer than ever before. More stay-at-home dads took primary responsibility for childcare. Lesbian and gay couples fought for—and increasingly won—the right to legally marry. Low-income women were working multiple jobs to keep food on their tables, feminists were advocating family leave and childcare policies, and middle- and upper-middle-class women were breaking barriers in business and government. The babes of "reality" TV? They just dreamed of cheerful, suburban dependence.

Mike Darnell, president of alternative entertainment at Fox, says his most successful reality shows are "steeped in some social belief." He's right. All this compulsory domesticity, this negating of individuality and will, rests on the underlying notion that women should think like '50s TV mom June Cleaver, screw like porn star Jenna Jameson, and look like Miss USA. It's a Donna Reed-meets-Pamela Anderson mashup, and ain't pretty. Despite how frivolous reality TV may seem or how much producers say it's all in good fun, the genre's psychological browbeating has political ramifications. These shows reinforce insecurities bred into women by decades of factually inaccurate news media reports of supposed "man shortages" and broken-down biological clocks, such as that infamous, landscape-shaping—and completely inaccurate—1986 *Newsweek* story that claimed that single women had a better chance of being killed by a terrorist than getting married after 40. Reality TV's wedding-industrial-complex shows insist we're doomed to unhappiness unless we rid ourselves of all traces of independence, ambition or—heaven forbid—feminist thought.

Darnell has said that he and other reality programmers just "give people what they want, pushing the envelope to match tastes." In fact, they're trying to *alter* our tastes, to convince us that 21st century Americans do not see women and men—or our society in general—much differently than we did before the women's rights and civil rights movements. Reality TV producers, embedded advertisers and media owners have done what the most ardent fundamentalists have never been able to achieve: They've created a universe in which women not only *have* no real choices—but don't even *want* any.

12

Reality TV Kids Need the Law on Their Side

Hilary Levey

Hilary Levey is a sociologist specializing in childhood and parenting at Harvard University. She has written extensively on children in the entertainment industry and in competitive events. She recently completed a book manuscript, Playing to Win: Raising Children in a Competitive Culture.

The increasingly common practice of parents seeking publicity, often in the form of a reality television contract, for their children places kids in danger of financial exploitation and a myriad of psychological issues. While a few states have passed laws protecting child performers, the current climate of exploitation requires far stricter measures to ensure that the child's well-being is of the highest priority.

Over the past weeks [in June of 2010] many have followed the saga of Abby Sunderland. At 16 years old, she was attempting to become the youngest person to sail solo around the world when a storm derailed her plans, resulting in an international search and rescue. Just two days after her rescue rumors of a reality show surfaced. *Adventures in Sunderland* would seem to be a surefire series—the devoutly Christian Sunderlands have seven homeschooled children (with another on the way), and their eldest son became the youngest person to circumnavigate the globe at 17. Sure enough, turns out dad Laurence signed a contract months ago to develop a show featuring his brood.

Sound familiar? Conspiracy theories started as comparisons were made to the Heene family, of "Balloon Boy" infamy. From families like the Gosselins (*Jon & Kate Plus Ei8ht*) to the Duggars (*19 Kids and Counting*), unusual families with multiple children produce ratings, and cash for their parents. But unless lawmakers step in to protect these children, this form of parental exploitation may end in tragedy.

The Sunderland story has eerie parallels to that of Jessica Dubroff: at 7, Jessica tried to become the youngest person to fly across the USA, an attempt that ended in tragedy as she, her father, and her flight instructor died in a crash. If reality television in 1996 had been what it is now, the Dubroffs likely would have been jones-ing for their own series, given their pursuit of publicity. Luckily, the Sunderland story has a happier ending.

Children on life's stage

I have spent the past decade studying children's competitive activities—from child beauty pageants to chess to soccer—and children's work, so I know that concerns about parental exploitation are nothing new. After making child labor, like factory work, illegal early in the 20th century, reformers tackled the problem of child performers. In 1939 California passed the Coogan law (named for famed child actor Jackie Coogan) to protect the earnings of young actors; today 15% of child performers' earnings must be placed in trust accounts. But only four states have Coogan laws—California and New York, where most child performers work, along with Louisiana and New Mexico. New Mexico passed their laws after controversy in 2007 when the CBS reality show *Kid Nation*, which featured 40 children and no adults, filmed near Sante Fe.

So what's different when it comes to kids and reality television? These kids are not classified as performers, denying them the protection of Coogan laws. In fact, the children are not even classified as workers, also denying them the protection of child labor laws. Kid reality stars fall through the cracks of the protections crafted by early 20th-century reformers, who likely never imagined that someone would consent to potty-training their children on camera (Season Three, Episode 4 of *Jon & Kate Plus Ei8ht*).

As reality television featuring kids continues to develop, legislators and lawyers need to step in to . . . protect the best interests of children.

Additionally, children's roles on shows that change their parents' lifestyles raise the question of whether parents should be the ones to consent to have their children filmed. These parents are famous for simply being parents in unusual families, a role they could not publicly play without the participation of their kids. They have a vested interest in making sure that five-figure per episode paychecks continue to arrive.

Lives in syndication

Also of concern are children's identities. Unlike, say, Miley Cyrus, who played the role of Hannah Montana, reality TV parents essentially consent for their children to "play" themselves. Children's personalities are dissected by viewers, and any embarrassing activities, like that potty training, are preserved on the Internet—or in syndication. The consequences of having to perform their identity for millions are simply unknown.

So, who "owns" a childhood, the child or the parents? At what age should a child's consent be required to have their lives edited and broadcast to millions? You can't have a Facebook account until you are 13, but 6-year-olds can be the "stars" of reality shows?

As reality television featuring kids continues to develop, legislators and lawyers need to step in to tackle these questions and protect the best interests of children. More states need to pass Coogan laws for all child performers, broadening the definition to include those performing as themselves. Earlier this month [June of 2010], Pennsylvania state Rep. Tom Murt proposed a bill that would offer protection to reality TV kids working there. The legislation limits the amount of hours kids can "work," gets teachers on "set," and protects children's earnings. Other states must follow suit.

Reality TV parents might be blinded by the lights of fame and tempted by the lure of riches. But they're adults. Their children shouldn't have to risk a lifetime of suffering to fulfill their parents' 15 minutes of fame.

13

Reality TV Producers Should Be Responsible for Participant Well-Being

Linda Holmes

Linda Holmes is the editor of the National Public Radio culture blog Monkey See. *A former attorney, she has written about television and pop culture at the blog* Television Without Pity *and has contributed articles to* TV Guide *and MSNBC.com.*

The psychological damage caused by being cast in a reality television show, brought into focus by the suicide of Real Housewives of Beverly Hills *participant Russell Armstrong, places a responsibility on reality TV producers to show more concern for the well-being of their subjects. While it would be difficult to mandate a code of ethics that all reality programs must abide by, allowing shows to opt in to such a code would give viewers the opportunity to support less exploitative reality programming.*

Unscripted television—now referred to as "reality" mostly so that people can put the word "reality" between appropriately skeptical quotation marks—has always been accused of being stupid, vapid, empty, and responsible for crowding out the good stuff that scripted television can accomplish.

Let's put that part aside.

Right now, the swelling chorus about this genre is not talking about long-term degradation of audience intelligence, but crises created for participants. What has put this on the front burner is the suicide [in 2011] of Russell Armstrong, the estranged husband of Taylor Armstrong, one of the women featured on Bravo's *The Real Housewives Of Beverly Hills*. His collapsing marriage was a major storyline on the show, which has an entire upcoming season in the can in which he plays a role. Bravo has decided to air the season, but has announced that there has been some re-editing, and that they'll air a special so everyone can talk about their feelings about it—everyone except his estranged wife.

In the aftermath of this developing horror show, Matt Zoller Seitz wrote a piece at *Salon*, and Andy Dehnart has published a feature in *Playboy* (which you really still *can* read for the articles, but be aware that your employer might not approve of the URL), about the potential hazards that can lie ahead when, as Matt Paxton of *Hoarders* says to Dehnart, "combine mental illness with entertainment."

There are ways for shows . . . to take their responsibilities to participants more seriously.

A Different Kind of Reality

As much as the purest solution (and the purist's solution) is to tell everyone to stop watching it entirely, any argument that it's unethical to watch entertainment that poses genuine risks to people would also take down football, boxing and the circus. That kind of entreaty may be justified, and can still be offered, but it will almost surely be ignored, and it's a bad idea to cling to it so fiercely that in the meantime, nothing else changes.

There is also, I'm sorry to say, no solution for people who want to watch *The Real Housewives Of Beverly Hills* without guilt—and I say that as someone who, while I don't watch that one, has watched the New York version. If you want to watch some of this stuff, you have to live with the fact that it exploits emotionally charged situations and could easily cause psychological harm to people, whether it was responsible for what happened to Russell Armstrong or not. The amount of risk you can live with is up to you (and has been very much on my own mind), and you don't necessarily have to feel worse than a football fan, but yes—know what you're into.

But just as responsible sports teams can make responsible decisions about minimizing risks where they can, there are ways for shows that absolutely *don't* have to be so exploitative and potentially damaging—shows like *Survivor* and *The Amazing Race* and *Project Runway* and *Top Chef* and even *American Idol* and *Deadliest Catch*—to take their responsibilities to participants more seriously and to distinguish and brand themselves as the shows committed to existing on the do-less-harm end of the spectrum. How do you accomplish that?

There are people who are not stupid, who don't love seeing people get hurt, who don't relish the idea of injury or emotional damage, . . . and would like to think basic protections are in place to protect people's well-being to the degree they can be.

With a voluntary, industry-adopted ethics code that would allow a show that wants to agree to specific measures that minimize (*do not* eliminate, but minimize) potential harm, and in return to be marketed as Not That Kind Of Show.

The fact that these measures would increase the costs of producing code-compliant shows is a feature, not a bug. You can spread some of the risks—which are currently dumped entirely on participants—to producers without making it unreasonably expensive to produce shows, *and* if a certain number of viewers decide they're going to favor code-compliant shows and a certain number of advertisers decide they're only going to advertise on code-compliant shows, some of those costs would be offset. It will ultimately be the responsibility of viewers and advertisers, in other words, to shop for ethical television the same way they might shop for ethically produced goods of any other kind, and to provide the financial incentives.

Meanwhile, everybody sleeps a little better. Just a little.

There would still be plenty of non-code shows—*Jersey Shore* isn't going to adopt any code of ethics, and its viewers aren't going to care—and plenty of networks to air them. But there are people who are not stupid, who don't love seeing people get hurt, who don't relish the idea of injury or emotional damage, who enjoy *Survivor* and *Project Runaway* and would like to think basic protections are in place to protect people's well-being to the degree they can be.

Small Measures, Big Impact

So, the nitty-gritty: What would such a code contain? Well, let's draft one. Some of these provisions are probably pipe dreams, some are utterly obvious, and most are—in my opinion as a longtime viewer and someone who has a few friends who have actually been on these shows—completely achievable for the vast majority of mainstream shows without damage to the product. . . . Again, nobody has to make their show this way if they don't want to, but every little bit helps.

It would be more expensive and it would close a few doors, and yes, some potential for exploitation drama would be sacrificed. But it would also prevent the baby of a perfectly good game show or documentary show from being thrown out with the bathwater of *The Real Housewives Of Beverly Hills*.

Here's what I'd ask of a code-compliant show.

Aftercare and counseling. Shows agree to provide up to three months of post-appearance counseling for any participant who requests it.

All contracts must be public. Shows agree that all contracts participants are asked to sign will be available on the show's web site.

Limitations on alcohol. Shows agree that producers will not use footage of participants who are intoxicated if the alcohol was provided by the producers.

Sleep requirements. Filming will be scheduled so as to allow at least six hours of uninterrupted sleep at least five nights out of every calendar week.

Minors. Shows agree to use no non-incidental footage of any child under age ten, and to employ an on-set counselor specializing in adolescents to provide care and advice on the well-being of any participant who is a minor.

Limits on isolation. Shows agree that participants who are removed to an unfamiliar environment that limits their contact with family, friends, or other important sources of support may choose one person with whom they may speak by telephone once a week for 10 minutes without penalty.

Medical care. Shows agree to provide participants with access to qualified physicians for any medical care they require during filming and to assume the costs of any care for an injury or illness that results from participation in the show. A participant who lacks confidence in the medical care he or she is receiving has the right to seek another opinion at his or her own expense without being penalized for any absence from filming.

Background checks. Shows agree to perform full background checks on participants who will reside with other participants outside their own homes and to disqualify any participant with any documented history of violence in the ten years prior to casting.

Repeat appearances. Because long-term participation has effects that short-term participation may not, shows agree that any appearance fee paid to a participant for a subsequent season of the same show must be at least three times the appearance fee for the first season in which the participant appeared. The appearance fee for subsequent seasons must be five times the original appearance fee.

Gag rules. Shows agree not to require participants to refrain from discussing their experiences in interviews subsequent to the conclusion of their participation.

Required follow-ups. Shows agree not to require participants to appear in reunion specials, follow-ups, speaking tours, or any other obligations that take place after the conclusion of principal filming.

Damage to reputation. Shows agree that their producers will participate once every three years in voting on the appointment of a three-person dispute resolution panel made up of individuals who are not employed in the production of television. Any participant who is required to sign a contract releasing a show from liability for intentional infliction of emotional distress or false light invasion of privacy has the right to bring complaints to that panel. Shows agree to provide up to three hours of raw footage requested by the complaining participant to the panel. If the panel concludes that the show materially misrepresented the participant's actions or character in a way that tends to substantially damage his or her reputation, the panel may require the show to make available online up to 30 minutes of raw footage that remedies the misrepresentation.

Incapacity. Shows agree that if a participant dies or is otherwise incapacitated while the show has in its possession any unaired footage of or referring to the person, no footage depicting or discussing the person will be shown unless the family of the person specifically requests that it be shown and no member of the person's immediate family requests that it not be shown.

Organizations to Contact

The editors have compiled the following list of organizations concerned with the issues debated in this book. The descriptions are derived from materials provided by the organizations. All have publications or information available for interested readers. The list was compiled on the date of publication of the present volume; names, addresses, phone and fax numbers, and e-mail and Internet addresses may change. Be aware that many organizations take several weeks or longer to respond to inquiries, so allow as much time as possible.

Academy of Television Arts & Sciences (ATAS)
5220 Lankershim Blvd., North Hollywood, CA 91601
(818) 754-2800
website: www.emmys.tv

The Academy of Television Arts & Sciences (ATAS) is a nonprofit corporation devoted both to the advancement of telecommunications arts and sciences and to fostering creative leadership in the telecommunications industry. It is the only major organization devoted to the television and broadband screen entertainment industry, and is made up of more than fifteen thousand members, representing twenty-eight professional peer groups, including performers, directors, producers, art directors and various other artisans, technicians, and executives. The Academy organizes the annual Daytime and Primetime Emmy Awards ceremonies honoring excellence in television programming and publishes *Emmy* magazine, a bimonthly publication featuring television-related news and editorial content.

Bunim/Murray Productions
6007 Sepulveda Blvd., Van Nuys, CA 91411
(818) 756-5150 • fax: (818) 756-5140
website: www.bunim-murray.com

Bunim/Murray Productions is widely acknowledged with creating the reality television genre with its hit series *The Real*

World (twenty-five seasons for MTV) in 1992. Bunim/Murray also created the first reality game show, *Road Rules* (MTV), in 1995; the first reality sitcom, *The Simple Life* (E!), in 2003; and the first reality soap opera, *Starting Over*, in 2003. The company publishes a regular e-mail newsletter featuring news about its reality shows, job opportunities, and casting calls for individuals interested in the industry.

Center for Media and Public Affairs (CMPA)
933 N. Kenmore St., Suite 405, Arlington, VA   22201
(571) 319-0034 • fax: (571) 319-0034
e-mail: mail@cmpa.com
website: www.cmpa.com

The Center for Media and Public Affairs (CMPA) is a nonpartisan research and educational organization affiliated with George Mason University that conducts scientific studies of news and entertainment media. CMPA's goal is to provide an empirical basis for ongoing debates over media coverage and impact through well-documented, timely, and readable studies. Its studies and findings are made available on its website.

Center for Research on the Effects of Television (CRETV)
119 Williams Hall, Ithaca, NY   14850-7290
(607) 274-1324 • fax: (607) 274-1925
e-mail: scheibe@ithaca.edu
website: www.ithaca.edu/cretv

The Center for Research on the Effects of Television (CRETV) is a television research and archival organization associated with Ithaca College that studies the influence of TV on a variety of subjects and demographics. CRETV has two components: an archive of television content and a research lab conducting studies of the content of television and its effects on viewers. The archive is used extensively by the CRETV researchers themselves and is also available as a resource for others. Analyses of the content are made available via the organization's website.

Directors Guild of America (DGA)
7920 Sunset Blvd., Los Angeles, CA   90046
(310) 289-2000
website: www.dga.org

Founded in 1936, the Directors Guild of America (DGA) is a labor organization that represents the creative and economic rights of directors and members of the directorial team working in film, television, commercials, documentaries, news, sports, and new media. In 2003, the DGA formed a special Reality TV Committee focusing on protecting rights, benefits, and compensation of reality TV directors. The committee publishes news and information about reality programs on the DGA website.

International Documentary Association (IDA)
1201 West 5th St., Suite M270, Los Angeles, CA   90017
(213) 534-3600
website: www.documentary.org

Founded in 1982, the International Documentary Association (IDA) is a nonprofit organization that promotes nonfiction filmmakers and is dedicated to increasing public awareness for the documentary genre. It publishes a monthly magazine, *Documentary*, and offers a number of articles and news items on its website. The association's annual West Coast Documentary and Reality Conference (WESTDOC) brings together the documentary and reality TV production communities to discuss techniques and strategies for nonfiction storytelling.

Media Watch
PO Box 618, Santa Cruz, CA   95061
(831) 423-6355
e-mail: info@mediawatch.com
website: www.mediawatch.com

Media Watch is an educational, nonprofit organization focusing on racism, sexism, and violence in media. It challenges abusive stereotypes and other biased information commonly found in the media through education and action. It publishes a monthly action newsletter and maintains a library of educational articles and videos on its website.

Minority Media & Telecommunications Council (MMTC)
3636 16th St. NW, Suite B-366, Washington, DC   20010
(202) 332-0500 • fax: (202) 332-0503
e-mail: info@mmtconline.org
website: http://mmtconline.org

The Minority Media & Telecommunications Council (MMTC) is a national nonprofit organization dedicated to promoting and preserving equal opportunity and civil rights in the mass media, telecommunications, and broadband industries. MMTC is the leading advocate for minority participation in the communications industries, seeking to preserve and expand minority ownership and equal employment opportunity in these industries. It publishes an annual report on the state of minority ownership of and representation on television and other broadcast media, and it maintains an ongoing Broadband and Social Justice Blog (BBSJ.org).

National Cable & Telecommunications Association (NCTA)
25 Massachusetts Ave. NW, Suite 100, Washington, DC   20001
(202) 222-2300
website: www.ncta.com

The NCTA is the principal trade association for the US cable industry, representing cable operators serving more than 90 percent of the nation's cable television households and more than two hundred cable program networks. It maintains a blog about current events related to the cable industry and presents the annual NCTA Vanguard Awards to innovative figures throughout the industry.

Nielsen Holdings N.V.
770 Broadway, New York, NY   10003-9595
website: www.nielsen.com

Nielsen is the primary ratings-tracking organization for television programs and online content, measuring the viewership of every program on TV via a sampling of representative households. It publishes regular ratings lists that are considered the authority on television viewership trends. Depending on the topic, Nielsen updates these lists on a weekly, monthly, or quarterly basis.

The Paley Center for Media
465 North Beverly Dr., Beverly Hills, CA   90210
(310) 786-1000
website: www.paleycenter.org

The Paley Center for Media encourages discussion about the cultural, creative, and social significance of television, radio, and emerging platforms among the professional community and media-interested public. It maintains a media collection of nearly 150,000 television and radio programs and advertisements at its Los Angeles and New York locations. It also conducts a number of public events exploring the relationship between the media and society via its media council and educational outreach programs.

Parents Television Council (PTC)
707 Wilshire Blvd. #2075, Los Angeles, CA   90017
(213) 403-1300 • fax: (213) 403-1301
e-mail: Editor@parentstv.org
website: www.parentstv.org

The Parents Television Council (PTC) is a US-based conservative advocacy group founded by conservative activist L. Brent Bozell III in 1995 using the National Legion of Decency as a model. Through publications on its website, including staff reviews, non-scientific research reports, and web-based newsletters, the council proclaims television programs or other entertainment products to be beneficial or harmful to the development of children. A number of its recent studies, including "Harsh Reality: Unscripted TV Reality Shows Offensive to Families" and "Reality of MTV: Gender Portrayals on Reality TV," focus specifically on reality TV shows.

Producers Guild of America (PGA)
8530 Wilshire Blvd. #400, Beverly Hills, CA   90211
(310) 358-9020
website: www.producersguild.org

The Producers Guild of America (PGA) is the nonprofit trade group that represents, protects, and promotes the interests of all members of the producing team in film, television, and new media. PGA has more than five thousand members who work together to protect and improve their careers, the industry, and community by facilitating members' health benefits, encouraging enforcement of workplace labor laws, and establishing fair and impartial standards for the awarding of producing credits, as well as other education and advocacy efforts. PGA hosts important industry events, including the annual PGA Awards and the Produced By Conference, and it publishes *Produced By* magazine, featuring industry news and profiles of prominent producers.

Reality TV World
PO Box 942, Mansfield, MA   02048
(206) 350-1418
e-mail: pr@realitytvworld.com
website: www.realitytvworld.com

Reality TV World is an independently operated web property that is the Internet's leading resource for reality television news and information. Providing coverage of nearly three hundred reality television programs, Reality TV World has been featured and cited by print, electronic, and online media sources, including outlets as diverse as CBS News, MTV, *TV Guide, Entertainment Weekly*, the *New York Times, USA Today*, and *Salon.*

Women's Media Center (WMC)
320 West 37th St., New York, NY   10018
(212) 563-0680 • fax: (212) 563-0688
e-mail: wmcny@womensmediacenter.com
website: www.womensmediacenter.com

The Women's Media Center (WMC) was founded in 2005 as a nonprofit progressive women's media organization by Jane Fonda, Robin Morgan, and Gloria Steinem to assure that women are included as sources for and subjects of the media, and that female media professionals are afforded equal opportunities for employment and advancement. It maintains a "media monitoring" division that publishes reports on sexism and gender issues in television and other media outlets.

Writers Guild of America, West (WGAw)
7000 West Third St., Los Angeles, CA   90048
(323) 951-4000 • fax: (323) 782-4800
website: www.wga.org

The Writers Guild of America, West (WGAw) is a labor union composed of the thousands of writers who write content for television shows, movies, news programs, documentaries, animation, and Internet and mobile phones (new media). In 2005, WGAw waged a "reality rights" campaign to extend benefits and protections to writers on reality programs, who are often classified as "story editors" or "story producers" rather than writers. In 2007, the Guild released a report on the treatment of reality TV writers titled "Harsh Reality: Working Conditions for Reality TV Writers," which is available on it's website. Other articles include "Why Reality Writers Ought to Be in the Guild" and "Unscripted Does Not Mean Unwritten."

Bibliography

Books

Mark Andrejevic   *Reality TV: The Work of Being Watched*. Lanham, MD: Rowman & Littlefield Publishers, 2004.

Sofie Bauwel and Nico Carpentier, eds.   *Trans-Reality Television: The Transgression of Reality, Genre, Politics, and Audience*. Lanham: Lexington Books, 2010.

Anita Biressi and Heather Nunn   *Reality TV: Realism and Revelation*. London: Wallflower Press, 2004.

Sam Brenton and Reuben Cohen   *Shooting People: Adventures in Reality TV*. London: Verso, 2003.

David S. Escoffery   *How Real Is Reality TV?: Essays on Representation and Truth*. Jefferson, NC: McFarland, 2006.

Michael Essany   *Reality Check: The Business and Art of Producing Reality TV*. Amsterdam: Focal Press/Elsevier, 2008.

Kevin Glynn   *Tabloid Culture: Trash Taste, Popular Power, and the Transformation of American Television*. Durham, NC: Duke University Press, 2000.

Annette Hill   *Reality TV: Audiences and Popular Factual Television*. London: Routledge, 2005.

Su Holmes and Deborah Jermyn, eds.   *Understanding Reality Television*. London: Routledge, 2004.

Richard M. Huff	*Reality Television.* Westport, CT: Praeger Publishers, 2006.
Richard Kilborn	*Staging the Real: Factual TV Programming in the Age of "Big Brother."* Manchester, UK: Manchester University Press, 2003.
Susan Murray and Laurie Ouellette, eds.	*Reality TV: Remaking Television Culture.* New York: New York University Press, 2009.
Laurie Ouellette and James Hay	*Better Living Through Reality TV: Television and Post-Welfare Citizenship.* Malden, MA: Blackwell, 2008.
Jennifer L. Pozner	*Reality Bites Back: The Troubling Truth About Guilty Pleasure TV.* Berkeley, CA: Seal Press, 2010.
Christopher Pullen	*Documenting Gay Men: Identity and Performance in Reality Television and Documentary Film.* Jefferson, NC: McFarland, 2007.
Beverley Skeggs and Helen Wood	*Reacting to Reality Television: Performance, Audience and Value.* New York: Routledge, 2012.
Matthew J. Smith and Andrew F. Wood, eds.	*Survivor Lessons: Essays on Communication and Reality Television.* Jefferson, NC: McFarland, 2003.
Julie A. Taddeo and Ken Dvorak, eds.	*The Tube Has Spoken: Reality TV & History.* Lexington: University Press of Kentucky, 2010.

Brenda R. Weber	*Makeover TV: Selfhood, Citizenship, and Celebrity*. Durham, NC: Duke University Press, 2009.
Wendy N. Wyatt and Kristie Bunton, eds.	*The Ethics of Reality TV: A Philosophical Examination*. New York: Continuum, 2012.

Periodicals and Internet Sources

Daniel Biltereyst	"Media Audiences and the Game of Controversy: On Reality TV, Moral Panic and Controversial Media Stories," *Journal of Media Practice*, June 2004.
Nicole B. Cox and Jennifer M. Proffitt	"The Housewives' Guide to Better Living: Promoting Consumption on Bravo's *The Real Housewives*," *Communication, Culture & Critique*, June 2012.
Kate Coyne	"*Kate Plus Eight*: 'My Family Can't Be Canceled,'" *People*, September 19, 2011.
Jan-Christopher Horak	"Wildlife Documentaries: From Classical Forms to Reality TV," *Film History*, Vol. 18, No. 4, 2006.
Chris Norris	"Hitting Bottom," *New York Times Magazine*, December 2010.
Helen Piper	"Reality TV, *Wife Swap* and the Drama of Banality," *Screen*, Winter 2004.

James Poniewozik and Jeanne McDowell	"How Reality TV Fakes It," *Time,* January 29, 2006.
Neal Saye	"No 'Survivors,' No 'American Idol,' No 'Road Rules' in the 'The Real World' of Big Brother: Consumer/Reality, Hyper/Reality, and Post/Reality in 'Reality' TV," *Studies in American Culture,* October 2004.
Camilla A. Sears and Rebecca Godderis	"Roar Like a Tiger on TV? Constructions of Women and Childbirth in Reality TV," *Feminist Media Studies,* Vol. 11, No. 2, 2011.
Tim Stack	"*Jersey Shore*: Skank You Very Much," *Entertainment Weekly,* July 24, 2010.
Graeme Turner	"The Mass Production of Celebrity: 'Celetoids', Reality TV and the 'Demonic Turn,'" *International Journal of Cultural Studies,* June 2006.
Junhow Wei	"Dealing with Reality: Market Demands, Artistic Integrity, and Identity Work in Reality Television Production," *Poetics,* October 2012.

Index